75
Chinese, Celtic, and Ornamental Knots

75
Chinese, Celtic, and Ornamental Knots

A directory of knots and knotting techniques—plus
exquisite jewelry projects to make and wear

●

LAURA WILLIAMS AND ELISE MANN

St. Martin's Griffin
New York

75 Chinese, Celtic, and Ornamental Knots
Copyright © 2011 Quarto, Inc.

www.stmartins.com

Library of Congress Cataloging-in-Publication data available on request.

ISBN: 978-0-312-67531-8

First U.S. Edition: January 2011

Conceived, designed, and produced by Quarto Publishing plc
The Old Brewery
6 Blundell Street
London N7 9BH

QUAR: DKJ

Senior Editor: Ruth Patrick
Art Editor and Designer: Julie Francis
Illustrator: Kuo Kang Chen
Photographer: Phil Wilkins
Art Director: Caroline Guest
Proofreader: Sally MacEachern
Indexer: Helen Snaith

Creative Director: Moira Clinch
Publisher: Paul Carslake

Color separation by Modern Age Pte Ltd
Printed in China by 1010 Printing International Ltd

10 9 8 7 6 5 4 3 2 1

Contents

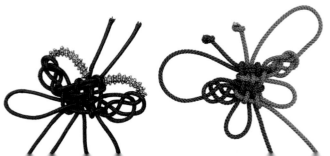

Foreword

Knots are useful, but they are also beautiful. For centuries, before buttons were used, they were used to hold clothing together, especially for those who could not afford metal pins, and the wearers wanted them to look as interesting as possible. More and more elaborate knots were created, some that would hold more strongly, but many that would simply look elegant or exotic. Knots became symbolic of protection, luck, and other good wishes, or of the wealth of the wearer when made with high-quality materials.

This book will show you how to tie many decorative knots, combine them to make still more elaborate pieces, and we hope, inspire you to incorporate them into many different jewelry pieces and other craft projects. We have provided some projects to give you some initial ideas and provide inspiration, but you will probably have other ideas, since there are almost unlimited possibilities to combine knots, use different materials, add beads and charms, and of course your imagination.

About this book

A comprehensive guide to creating and using knots in jewelry-making, study the core techniques before choosing from the directory of 75 knots, organized into Eastern and Western styles. The projects at the end of the book demonstrate how to use the knots in jewelry projects.

Materials, tools, and techniques (pages 8–19)

This part describes all the necessary equipment and outlines the core techniques you will need to create beautiful knotted jewelry, from tying, tightening, and sealing knots to attaching jump rings and other findings.

Step-by-step sequences
Step-by-step instructions walk you through the methods.

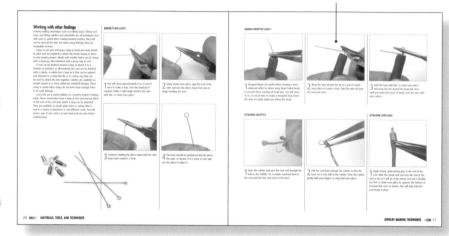

Knot selector (pages 24–27)

Turn to the Knot selector to see all the knots laid out next to each other over four pages, make comparisons, and select the one you want to work.

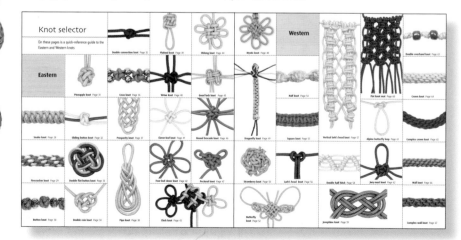

Directory of knots (pages 22–107)

The knot directory contains 75 knots, organized into Eastern and Western styles, with detailed step-by-step instructions to show how to tie them.

Sample from the Eastern knots section

Lengths given for each knot are approximate and based on 2-mm Korean knotting cord. Thicker or less flexible cords may require more length; thinner or softer cords will need less.

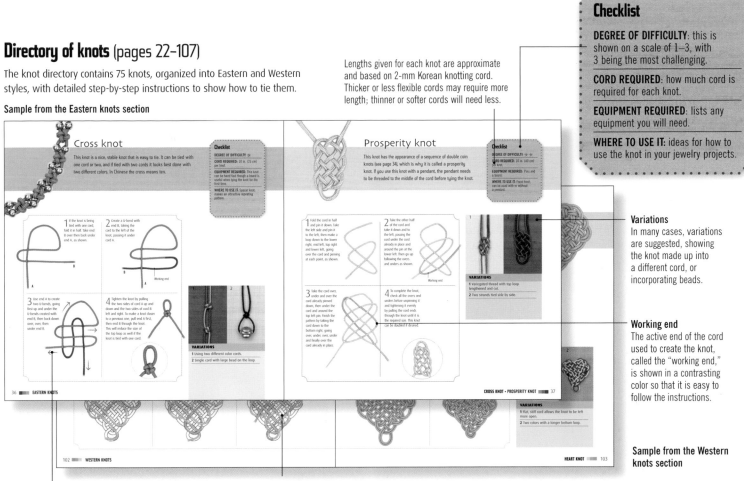

Variations
In many cases, variations are suggested, showing the knot made up into a different cord, or incorporating beads.

Working end
The active end of the cord used to create the knot, called the "working end," is shown in a contrasting color so that it is easy to follow the instructions.

Sample from the Western knots section

Arrows
Where relevant, arrows show the directions in which the cords should be pulled in order to tighten the knot.

Templates
Templates are supplied where needed.

Jewelry projects (pages 108–123)

A range of jewelry projects for different skill levels lets you put your new-found skills into practice.

Materials
Lists the tools and materials you will need.

Step-by-step instructions

Finished project

Materials, tools, and techniques

The right tools and materials make learning new knots and creating beautiful finished work much easier. Practice basic techniques so that you are confident when you need to use them.

Materials for knotting

Almost any type of cord can be used for knotting, but some, such as yarns and fluffy chenille strands, will not show the work clearly. Different cords have different properties, so it is worth considering the options before starting any project.

Cords

Cord is the most important material for creating knotted jewelry. Sometimes it is the only material required. There are many different types of cord that can be used to tie ornamental knots, though some types are better suited to certain knots than others. Larger, ornamental knots, particularly those with loops, need to be tied with a wider-diameter cord that is fairly rigid to ensure the knot pattern is visible for all to see and that it retains its shape. Smaller knots that are tied in sequence to create braids and plaits can be tied with narrower, more pliable cords as the sequence of knots will create an overall pattern and hold the individual knots together.

Cords are available in a wide variety of diameters, depending on the type of cord chosen. Cords between 1mm and 2mm diameter are best for knotted jewelry, and novice knot tiers are better off using thicker cord to start with as it is easier to see what you're doing.

A fantastic range of colors is available for most cord types, particularly the satiny cord, rattail, and the Korean knotting cord used throughout most of this book. Even leather is available in a fairly wide variety of colors. Some cords are available in a variegated effect, with the cord changing color along its length. This sort of cord creates a nice effect when used to tie some of the simpler knots, when only one cord is used, but it is best avoided when tying larger, more intricate knots as it detracts from the natural pattern and shape of the knot. The same guidelines apply when using textured cord.

When selecting cords, choose one that is flexible enough to tie, rigid enough to hold its shape, comes in a color suited to your jewelry project, and is in a diameter large enough to show off your handiwork.

1 LEATHER

Leather comes in a fairly wide range of colors and in 1-mm, 1.5-mm, and 2-mm diameters. Leather is a good cord for tying knots that don't require a lot of manipulation or excessive tightening, as too much manipulation can damage the cord. Leather is ideal for creating jewelry for men as it has a masculine feel to it.

2 HEMP OR JUTE

Hemp is a natural fiber and is therefore a nice cord to combine with semiprecious beads to create jewelry with an "eco-friendly," natural look. It ties and tightens easily but is too pliable for large, ornamental knots with loops as it will not hold the loops. It is available in 0.5-mm and 1-mm widths in a wide variety of colors, though it suits pastel and neutral shades. The same applies to jute, often sold as garden twine, although it is a little hairy.

3 STRING

Simple string bought from stationery stores is an excellent material for practicing knotting as it is soft enough to manipulate easily but rigid enough to hold its shape. It is also cheap to buy.

4 RATTAIL

Rattail is a satiny cord made of rayon. Rattail is available in 2-mm diameter, 1.5-mm diameter (called mousetail) and 1-mm diameter (called bugtail), though the 2mm seems to be the easiest width to get hold of. It is available in a wide variety of bright, pastel, and variegated colors. It is a shiny, slippery cord that makes it easy to tie, tighten, and manipulate. This does mean that some knots tied with rattail need a stitch to keep them in shape. It is suitable for tying most knots and looks particularly attractive when tying Eastern knots.

5 KOREAN KNOTTING CORD

This cord is the one used throughout most of this book. It is available in both 1.5-mm and 2-mm widths and is particularly good for tying larger, loose looped knots as it is rigid enough to hold its shape well. It ties and tightens easily, standing up well to lots of manipulation. It is available in a wide range of pastel and bright colors. It is made of a braided rayon cord woven around a cotton inner core.

1

2

3

4

6 COTTON

Cotton cord is a waxed cord and is available in a range of diameters from 0.5mm up to 3mm. As this cord is a natural cord it looks good in neutral colors but it is available in a small selection of brighter colors too. Use to tie simpler knots, particularly plaits or braids, and combine with beads. It doesn't stretch and tightens well but withstands only moderate manipulation.

7 SYNTHETIC SUEDE

Suede is a ribbon style cord that is 3mm wide and about 1mm deep. It is available in a small range of colors, mostly pale, neutral ones. It is a nicely textured cord so is better suited to simpler knots. It ties well but does not cope well with lots of handling. It can also be quite stretchy and shouldn't be allowed to get wet.

8 METALLIC CORD

Available on reels from craft suppliers, metallic cord is available in various thicknesses. It knots well but is quite easily damaged by too much manipulation.

9 EMBROIDERY THREAD

Embroidery thread is a 6- or 8-ply cord that is about 1mm thick and comes in a massive range of colors, including variegated and metallic. It can be doubled up and plaited or braided but isn't suitable for much more than that as the knots created are just too small to see!

10 FLOWER THREAD

A thicker thread also used for embroidery but rather firmer and so able to make more visible knots.

11 UPHOLSTERY CORDS

Twisted cords and braids sold for upholstery can be useful for simple knots where a larger result is required for a feature, but beware as they can detract from the details of the knot.

12 FLAT BRAID

Flattened cords or braids to sew onto clothes or decorate household items can be used for heavier results, and work especially well for complex looped knots as they are quite rigid. Be careful to keep the braid flat as you work as it will not pull through to tighten if it is twisted.

13 WIRE

Wire obviously isn't a cord but it can create a classic look and stylish jewelry. There are a variety of widths available, often described as gauges. 24-gauge (0.5mm) and 22-gauge (0.6mm) wires are good general-purpose sizes. Wire is available in different colors as well as the more usual gold, silver, or copper. Knots tied in wire will not be as even or as tight as those tied with cord, and metal wire becomes more brittle with use but it is worth trying wire for something a little different.

CHINESE KNOTTING CORD

Chinese knotting cord is a round, braided nylon cord. It is available in 0.8-mm and 1.5-mm diameters and in a wide variety of colors. It is easy to work with, withstanding manipulation, and ties and tightens well. It is a fairly rigid cord and due to its braided texture it holds its shape well so is suitable for use with the larger looped knots, though maybe on a more delicate scale to the smaller-diameter cord.

NYLON

Nylon, or parachute, cord comes in a wide range of diameters, though the 1mm, 1.5mm, and 2mm are most useful for jewelry-making. It is available from hardware stores or on-line. It is readily available in white but takes easily to being dyed with a multipurpose fabric dye. This can be done in the microwave and means an almost infinite number of colors can be created. It is easy to tie and holds its shape well. It also withstands a lot of manipulation so is well suited to complex knots that require a lot of tightening.

Other materials and tools

There are many knots that can be tied easily in your hands, and in some cultures, particularly Korean, all knots were traditionally tied purely in the hands, with no other tools to aid tying. However, the majority of knots are easier to tie with a little help, even if it is simply a safety pin to attach the end of your braiding to an anchor point.

Tools

When choosing materials and equipment to aid your knotted jewelry-making, choose the best you can afford. Good-quality equipment will last longer and make knot-tying easier and more efficient. Don't be tempted to struggle tying complex knots without the help of the minimum of a board and pins. You will only end up in a tangled mess and be disheartened and quite likely put off tying knots forever!

One of the best things about creating jewelry with ornamental knots is the simplicity and lack of specialized equipment required. Most of the items described can be purchased from craft, notions, or hardware stores so are very easy to get hold of. Anything you cannot find locally will be available on the Internet.

1 CORK BOARD

A cork board is an essential piece of equipment for tying larger ornamental knots. A knot is laid out flat and pinned down to ensure the overs and unders of the cord are correct so the knot tightens correctly. Make sure your board is large enough, at least the size of an U.S. letter (A4) piece of paper and at least ½ in. (1 cm) thick. If you can't find a cork board or cork tiles, a thick piece of corrugated cardboard will also work.

2 PINS

Pins are essential to hold your knotting flat and keep it in the correct shape. Dressmaking and lace pins work best as they are sharp and fine enough not to damage the cord when piercing it. Choose pins with wide heads. T-pins are available with bars on the top and dressmaking pins are available with round, plastic heads. These will stop you from hurting your fingertips pushing pins into the board.

3 NEEDLES

Sometimes the larger knots require a little stitch or two to stop them undoing, particularly if tied with slippery cord, so a fine needle and thread are required for this. To complete a necklace or bracelet, you may sometimes have to pull the cords back through a knot, and a large-eyed tapestry needle makes this easier.

4 MEASURING TAPE

Measuring tape or a ruler is required to measure the cord before you begin to make jewelry. It is also useful for deciding the required finished length of a piece of jewelry before starting.

5 LIGHTER

A disposable lighter, available from convenience or grocery stores, can be used to seal synthetic cord ends (see page 17).

6 SCISSORS

Make sure your scissors are sharp and cut your cords diagonally to create a pointed end. This will make it easier to thread the ends through beads. Use cord-cutting scissors only for cutting cord. You will leave a sticky residue on them if you use them to cut sticky tape that will stop cord cutting cleanly in the future.

PVA GLUE

PVA should be diluted one part glue to 10 parts water and then applied to stiffen large, open knots. It can also be used undiluted to seal cord ends. Apply it with a paintbrush.

STICKY TAPE

Sticky tape—either masking tape or clear tape—can be used to seal cord ends before knotting.

QUICK GLUE (SUCH AS EPOXY RESIN)

This is useful for two purposes. One is to glue the ends of cords to the back of a knot out of the way when completing a piece of jewelry. It can also be used, if required, for gluing beads in place if they are not held there by knots.

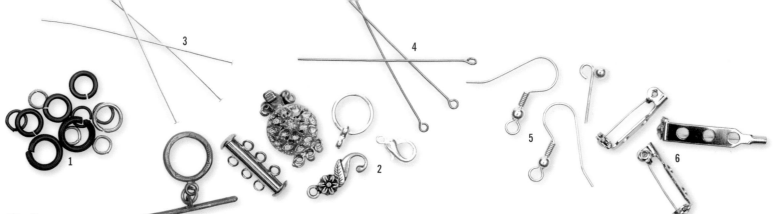

Findings

Knotted jewelry does not require a lot of findings as knots can often be used as clasps. Sliding button knots (see page 32) can be used to lengthen and tighten a necklace after sliding it over your head, and bracelets can simply be tied around the wrist. However, sometimes a clasp will be required and some beads will need to be attached with jump rings or hung on head or eye pins.

Findings are available in a range of materials, such as copper, silver, and gold, and the cheaper gold- and silver-plated alternatives. The purity of gold is described as karats—9-karat gold contains 9 parts gold to 15 parts other metals, through to 22-karat gold that contains 22 parts gold to 2 parts other metals. Pure gold and pure silver are described as fine gold and silver. Sterling silver and gold over silver are cheaper good-quality alternatives to the pure metals and are better quality than gold- and silver-plated findings which can lose their plating with time.

Like beads, choose findings that suit your jewelry. Chunky clasps often look better due to the sizes of the cords. Ensure the holes for fitting the clasps are large enough to fit your cord through and that the metal of the clasp suits the cord colors used. Cool colors, such as blue and purple, look stylish with silver findings, whereas gold suits warm oranges and reds. Findings are available from local craft stores and on-line. Look for something different to add originality to your jewelry.

1 JUMP RINGS

Jump rings are metal rings that can be pried opened and closed to join, for instance, a clasp and a length of chain together. They come in different diameters, thicknesses, and materials, including brightly colored aluminum.

2 CLASPS

There is a huge range of clasps available for use in jewelry-making. They range from the simple lobster trigger clasp to the two-part clasps, such as the toggle clasp. Toggle clasps consist of a ring that attaches to one end of a necklace or bracelet and a bar that attaches to the other end that fits through the ring to act as a fastener.

3 HEAD PINS

Head pins are thin metal bars with a flattened end that are used to string beads onto. They are not usually used with knotted jewelry but may be required if you wish to combine bead stringing with knots. A loop at the end of the pin will need to be made to attach the strung beads to your jewelry.

4 EYE PINS

Eye pins have the same use as head pins but have a loop in one end rather than a flat end. This loop can be opened to attach eye pins strung with beads together. Both head and eye pins come in different lengths and metals.

5 EAR WIRES

Ear wires are essential when making dangly earrings. They have a loop at the bottom which is opened to fit the earring onto it. Ear wires are available in different metals. The purer forms of gold and silver are least likely to cause sensitivity.

6 BROOCH BACKS

Celtic knots such as the heart knot (see page 102) are flat knots so lend themselves well to being turned into brooches. All they need is the addition of a brooch back. Brooch backs come in different lengths.

7 CORD END FITTINGS

These fit onto the end of a cord to give a loop to attach further findings. They come in different widths to fit narrow or wider cords. Some are solid and others can be crushed to hold the cord more firmly.

8 KEYRINGS

Keyring split rings can be purchased with or without chains. They are available in different sizes and shapes, as well as the usual round. Ornamental knots, particularly ones of Eastern origins, are thought to bring good luck, so why not create a good luck charm for a friend to use as a keyring or handbag charm.

9 CELL PHONE STRAPS

These looped straps loop through the holes in some cell phones to create a quick and easy phone charm. Like a keyring, a single knot attached with a jump ring to a cell phone strap makes an original good luck charm for you or a friend.

CALOTTES

These fit onto the end of a cord, creating a loop to which you can attach other findings (see page 21).

Beads

Ornamental knots are beautiful in themselves and some knotted jewelry is complete with just knots, however, the inclusion of beads can make an excellent addition to knotted jewelry.

Beads come in a huge array of colors, shapes, sizes, and materials. Beads can be made from bone, wood, acrylic, ceramic, glass, metals such as silver and gold, polymer clay, precious metal clay and semiprecious stones. You can even get beads made from paper and textiles.

When choosing beads for your knotted jewelry make sure they suit your project. If you're using thick cord, choose chunky beads; for finer cords, choose more delicate beads. If you're using a natural cord in neutral colors, such as hemp, use a natural-looking bead, such as a semiprecious stone, rather than a bright, plasticky-looking bead. Also, match the beads to the knots. Lots of large beads with large, complex knots can look a bit overcrowded so pair large knots with delicate beads or a large beautiful pendant with simple braided knots.

Beads are available from local craft stores, on-line, and also specialized bead fairs, which are great to go to if there is one in your area. Look out for handmade beads as these will create a truly original piece of jewelry when teamed with your hand-tied knots.

Bead hole size

The most important factor when choosing beads is the hole size. Due to most cords being at least 1mm thick you will need to ensure the cord fits through the beads. There is little point in buying beautiful beads that you are unable to use because your cord is too thick to pass through the holes. Try a selection of beads with the cord to be used as not all beads have uniform-sized holes.

• 1mm
• 1.5mm
• 2mm
• 2.5mm
• 3mm
• 3.5mm
• 4mm

1 BONE/HORN/WOOD

Bone and wooden beads look really great teamed with natural cords to create natural, earthy jewelry. There is a wide variety of sizes and shapes available and bone-carved pendants are very attractive. Wooden beads are available in a variety of colors, often natural, and can be quite chunky.

2 METAL

Metal beads can be gold, silver, brass, copper, and pewter, among others. Metal pendants are often available, sometimes combined with stones or crystals. Metal beads are often spacer beads, small, round, or flat beads, often textured or patterned, that sit in between larger beads or knots.

3 GLASS/LAMPWORK

There is a huge range of glass beads available, including striking pendants. Lampwork beads are handmade using rods of glass that are melted around a mandrel to create shapes and textures. No two beads are alike and they are ideally suited to hand-knotted jewelry.

4 CERAMIC

Made of china or porcelain, some ceramic beads have big holes as they are made on large rods or pierced with thick drills when the clay is still unfired.

5 METAL CLAY

Metal clay is clay made of metal particles, an organic binder, and water. The most common is silver clay. The clay is molded to the desired shape, dried and then heated in a kiln. This firing process burns off the binder, leaving a product that is 99% silver, so can be called fine (pure) silver. There are many craft workers making metal clay beads and pendants, and these handmade beads are the perfect complement to knotted jewelry.

6 POLYMER CLAY

Polymer clay is a plastic modeling material. It is hardened at low temperatures and can be used to create pretty much anything! It comes in a wide range of colors and textures and can be shaped by pressing textured items into it. Polymer clay beads are available in many shapes and sizes, from simple rounds to cupcakes!

7 TEXTILE

Textile beads are often chunky with large holes and are usually very colorful. Fabric-covered beads are available in a variety of patterns and colors. There are crochet beads, woven beads, and wound-cord beads. Felt balls are also available; these need to be pierced with a bead reamer or large needle to create a hole.

8 PAPER

Paper beads are normally made from strips of recycled colored paper, such as magazines, which are then rolled and varnished. Many paper beads available are made in poorer countries and purchased under Fair Trade agreements, creating an income for the manufacturers and ethically purchased beads for the buyer. They are available in a wide range of colors and sizes. Check the hole sizes as they will not be uniform.

9 ACRYLIC

Plastic beads are available in a wide range of colors, sizes, and shapes, including objects such as flowers or stars. They are also available in different textures and finishes and the opaque ones look attractive with colored cord. They often come in large packs and are an economical option.

10 SEMIPRECIOUS

Semiprecious beads are made from semiprecious stones. They are beautiful beads and a lot of the stones have healing powers attributed to them. For instance, Rose Quartz is believed to encourage peace, fidelity, and happiness and enhances self-confidence and creativity. Many are also birth stones so can be used to create a birthday gift for a special person. Check hole sizes on semiprecious beads as they are hard beads and it isn't easy to make the holes bigger.

Knotting techniques

Practice the basic techniques, such as tying and tightening on simple knots, with easy cords before attempting the more interesting (and more complex) varieties. Finishing the ends can also make knotting easier.

Tying knots

Some knots are harder to tie than others. The knots in this book have a difficulty rating and it is best to start off with the simpler knots. Once you have mastered tying and tightening the simpler knots, the more complex ones will be easier to create.

The easiest way to tie more complex ornamental knots is on a cork board using pins to keep the shape of the knot correct. Eventually you will be able to tie some knots in your hands without the aid of a cork board and pins. When first starting out tying knots use more cord than is recommended. This will prevent you struggling with a cord that you find too short or ending up with an uneven knot with some parts tighter than others.

Before creating jewelry with ornamental knots ensure you are familiar with how the knots are tied and practice simply tying the knots before incorporating them in a jewelry project.

Making a photocopy of the knot pattern and then pinning it to your cork board is a simple visual way to follow the pattern of a complex knot.

Many knots are similar in the way they are tied, so mastering one makes it easier to master another similar one. The crown and wall knots are tied in a similar way despite creating different effects. Celtic knots all follow a repeating over-and-under pattern so the method of tying remains the same, regardless of the size and apparent complexity of the knot.

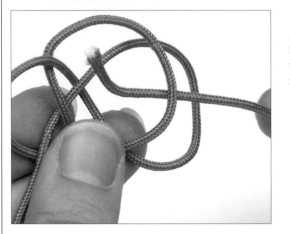

1 Shape the loops on a board and pin them down so that you can easily see where the next part has to be placed. This can be very helpful when you are practicing, and is necessary for some of the more complex knots even when you are experienced.

2 Many knots can be tied in the hand once you know the sequence and have confidence in your ability to hold the loops in the right pattern. This is the same knot as shown pinned above.

Tightening knots

Tightening knots correctly determines the final shape and look of a knot. When tightening knots that have already been tied, start tightening at the point where the knot was started. Tighten slowly and carefully, a little at a time, and always work in the same direction around the knot. If the knot is tied with more than one cord, work with one cord at a time, following each cord around the path of the knot. When first tying knots using two or more cords, it can be easier to use different colors to avoid confusion over which cord you are working with when tying and tightening.

When tightening knots with loops, some will loosen in the center when changing the sizes of the loops, so ensure you keep hold of the center of the knot to stop it unraveling.

If you are tightening knots that have been doubled or tripled with separate cords, then they can all be tightened as one cord but if you've used the same cord to double or triple the knot, the cord will have to be pulled round the knot more than once to tighten it. The most important thing to remember when tightening knots is to work slowly and methodically.

1 Many macramé knots, especially those used repeatedly to form fancy cords, must be tightened as you go. These knots need to be tightened evenly, ensuring the beginning is as tight as the end to keep the look of the knotting even throughout.

2 Other knots, such as most of the Eastern knots, the mats, and the Celtic knots, must be loosely tied and then tightened by gradually pulling the sections toward the ends.

Sealing cords

Cord ends that haven't been sealed are likely to fray, making it harder to tie the knots as the cord doesn't fit neatly through the holes in the knot pattern and makes attaching beads difficult. Sealed cords also look neater. Cords need to be sealed before any knotting is started and then the knot needs to be finished off neatly to hide loose cord ends, sometimes requiring further sealing.

To make sealing cord ends easier, cut the cord diagonally. When sealed, the cord will have a hard tip, which makes knotting and beading easier.

When choosing a method to seal your cords, remember that different methods suit different projects. Sealing cords with sticky tape will make your cord a little wider, so isn't suitable if the holes in your beads are only just wide enough for the cord to fit through. When using glue, you will have to wait for it to dry or your cord will stick to itself when you are tying knots. Sealing with glue is the best method if you are working with irregular-size bead holes as the glue creates a very hard end. Sealing cords with a flame only works on manmade cords. This method is best suited to projects containing only knots and no beads, as it only seals the very tip of the cord.

SEALING CORDS WITH A FLAME

1 Cords can be sealed with the flame from a disposable lighter. Hold the end of the cord in the flame for a fraction of a second.

2 This method works with most manmade fibers and seals only about 3mm at the end of the cord. Flame sealing can be used to seal trimmed ends when knotting is complete.

SEALING CORDS WITH STICKY TAPE

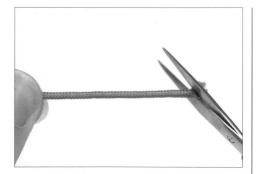

1 Cut the cord diagonally to produce a pointed end.

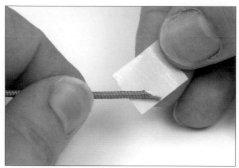

2 Cut a small piece of sticky tape and place the corner of the tape under the cord.

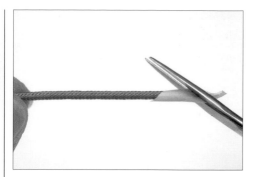

3 Roll the tape around the cord. The bigger the piece of tape used, the more cord will be covered. Trim the end of the cord to cut off the overhanging bit of sticky tape.

SEALING CORDS WITH GLUE

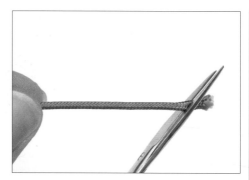

1 Cut the cord diagonally to produce a pointed end.

2 Using a paintbrush, paint undiluted PVA glue over the cord end. Make sure the whole cord end is completely covered up to an inch (2.5cm) from the end.

3 Prop the end of the cord and allow it to dry for at least an hour. When dry, trim the end to create a hard, sharp point.

Jewelry-making techniques

Although you do not need a lot of complex jewelry-making techniques for knotted work, it is useful to know a few basics so that you can easily attach findings to your projects.

Attaching jump rings

Jump rings are small metal rings that need to be opened before attaching things to them and closing again. Jump rings come in a wide variety of materials, such as silver and gold, their plated alternatives, and aluminum and copper. Aluminum and copper jump rings are available in different colors. These anodized jump rings come in bright colors such as blue, red, turquoise, pink, purple, and orange. Jump rings come in many diameters and thicknesses so the inner diameters vary too.

Silver and gold and their plated versions are readily available from craft and bead stores, and colored jump rings are available on-line from web sites that supply products for chain mail.

Pliers are required to open and close jump rings. Often available in kits from craft stores, pliers come in flat-nose, round-nose, and chain-nose varieties. Flat-nose pliers have flat jaws with squared-off ends. They are used to flatten wire and to hold items steady while working on them. Round-nose pliers have rounded, tapered jaws. They are useful for shaping wire and creating loops in head pins. Chain-nose pliers are tapered to a point but are flat on the inside surface. Always use tools specifically made for jewelry-making, as other types of pliers may have rough surfaces that will mark the wire.

You can even make your own jump rings by wrapping wire around, for example, a knitting needle, to create the desired diameter to make a spring. Slide the spring off the knitting needle, then cut through the wire with sharp wire cutters. You will end up with already opened jump rings.

When working with colored jump rings, if you find that they mark easily, either use nylon jaw pliers or wrap masking tape around your usual pliers to prevent them scratching the surface of plated jump rings and removing the color.

1 Hold the jump ring on either side of the opening using two pairs of pliers.

2 Do not pull the ring apart as this will distort the shape and the ring will not close properly again. Use one pair of pliers to hold the jump ring and the other to push the other half of the ring backward.

3 Attach the clasp, cord, beads, or other jump ring, then close the ring.

Round-nose pliers

Chain-nose pliers

Flat-nose pliers

Working with other findings

Jewelry-making techniques such as making loops, fitting cord ends, and fitting calottes and clamshells are all techniques that will come in useful when making knotted jewelry. They will not be used all the time but when using findings they are invaluable to learn.

Loops in eye pins and loops made in head pins keep beads in place and are required to attach the beads strung on them to your jewelry project. Beads with smaller holes can be strung onto a head pin, then attached with a jump ring to cord.

A cord can be knotted around a clasp to attach it to a bracelet or necklace, or alternatively the cord can be finished with a calotte. A calotte has a loop on it that can be opened and attached to a clasp directly or to a jump ring that can be used to attach the two together. Calottes are available as simple rounds or as more elaborate clamshell designs. These come in useful when clasps do not have large enough holes to fit cords through.

Cord ends are a useful addition to a jewelry maker's findings stash. These metal tubes have a loop at one end and are fitted to the end of the cord onto which a clasp can be attached. They are available as simple plain tubes or spring effects and in a variety of diameters to suit different cords. You will need a pair of side cutters to trim head and eye pins before making loops.

MAKING PLAIN LOOPS

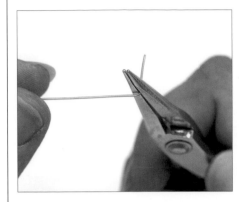

1 You will need approximately ½ in. (1 cm) of wire to make a loop. Trim the head pin if required. Make a right-angle bend in the wire with flat- or chain-nose pliers.

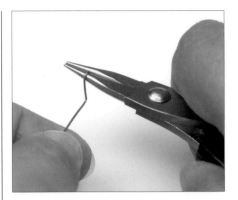

2 Using round-nose pliers, grip the end of the wire and turn the pliers away from you to begin bending the wire.

3 Continue rotating the pliers round until the wire loops back round in a circle.

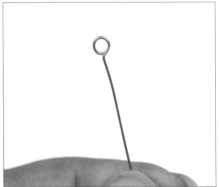

4 The loop should be positioned directly above the wire, as shown. If it is more to one side, use the pliers to adjust it.

MAKING WRAPPED LOOPS

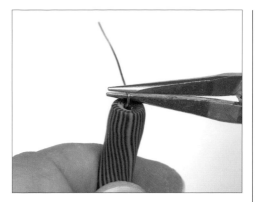

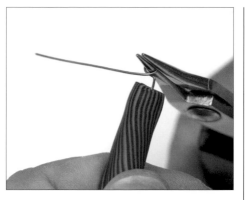

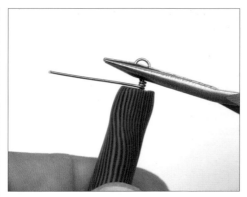

1 Wrapped loops are useful when creating a more elaborate effect or when using larger holed beads to prevent them coming off head pins. You will need 1¼ in. (3 cm) of wire to create a wrapped loop. Bend the wire at a right angle just above the bead.

2 Wrap the wire around the tip of a pair of round-nose pliers to create a loop. Take the wire tail past the head pin stem.

3 Hold the loop with flat- or chain-nose pliers and wrap the tail around the head pin stem until you reach the bead. To finish, trim the wire with wire cutters.

ATTACHING CALOTTES

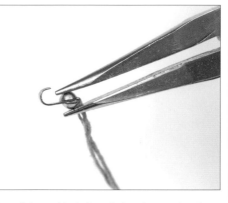

1 Open the calotte and pass the cord end through the hole in the middle. Tie a simple overhand knot in the cord and trim the end close to the knot.

2 Pull the cord back through the calotte so that the knot sits in one half of the calotte. Close the calotte gently with your fingers or using flat-nose pliers.

ATTACHING CORD ENDS

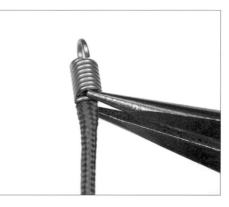

1 Apply strong, quick-drying glue to the end of the cord. Slide the metal cord end over the end of the cord as far as it will go. If the metal cord end is flexible, use flat- or chain-nose pliers to squeeze the bottom of it around the cord, as shown. This will help hold the cord firmly in place.

Directory of knots

The directory is split into two sections: Eastern knots mainly based on Chinese traditions; and Western knots mainly based on macramé and Celtic knot patterns. Both have variations and combination knots too.

Knot selector

On these pages is a quick-reference guide to the Eastern and Western knots

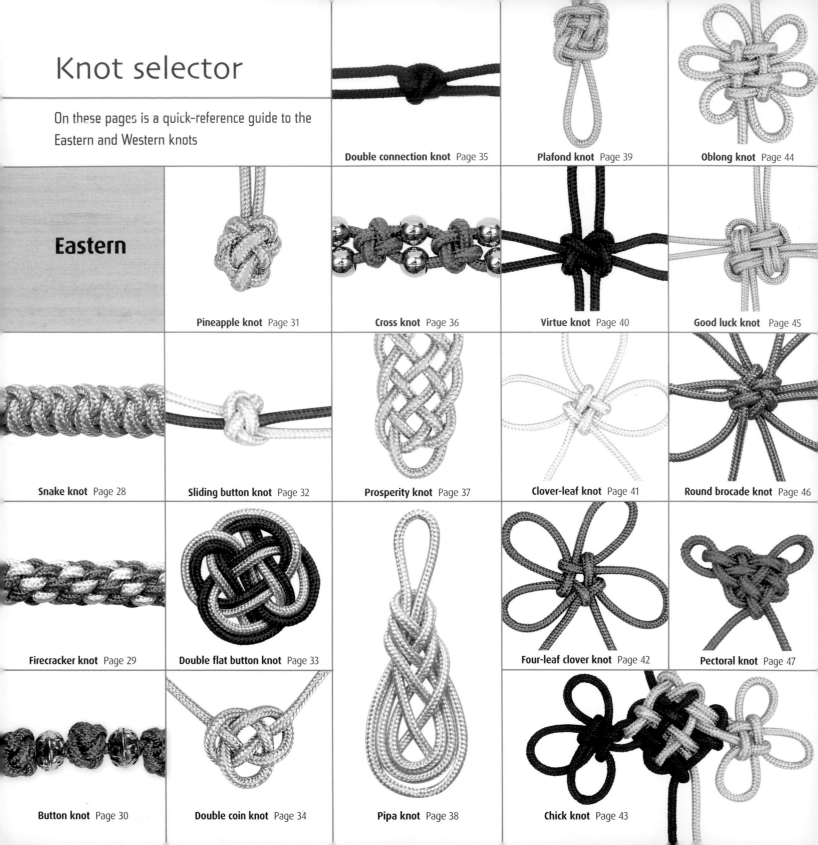

Double connection knot Page 35

Plafond knot Page 39

Oblong knot Page 44

Eastern

Pineapple knot Page 31

Cross knot Page 36

Virtue knot Page 40

Good luck knot Page 45

Snake knot Page 28

Sliding button knot Page 32

Prosperity knot Page 37

Clover-leaf knot Page 41

Round brocade knot Page 46

Firecracker knot Page 29

Double flat button knot Page 33

Four-leaf clover knot Page 42

Pectoral knot Page 47

Button knot Page 30

Double coin knot Page 34

Pipa knot Page 38

Chick knot Page 43

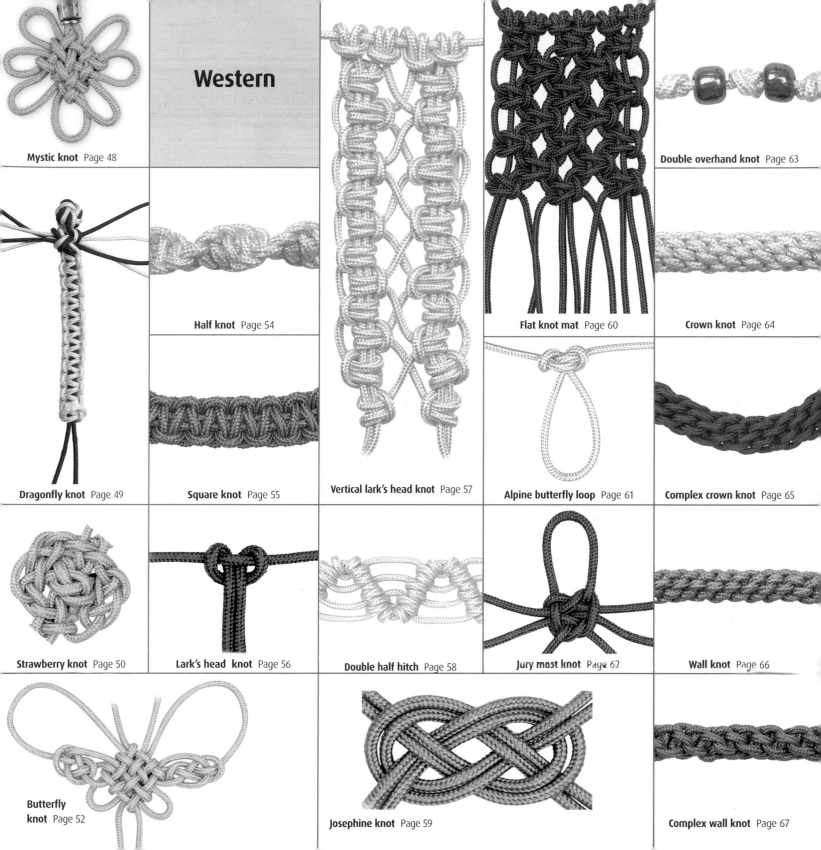

Mystic knot Page 48

Western

Double overhand knot Page 63

Half knot Page 54

Flat knot mat Page 60

Crown knot Page 64

Dragonfly knot Page 49

Square knot Page 55

Vertical lark's head knot Page 57

Alpine butterfly loop Page 61

Complex crown knot Page 65

Strawberry knot Page 50

Lark's head knot Page 56

Double half hitch Page 58

Jury mast knot Page 62

Wall knot Page 66

Butterfly knot Page 52

Josephine knot Page 59

Complex wall knot Page 67

Epaulette knot Page 68

Manrope knot Page 71

Four-lead, five-bight Turk's head knot Page 76

Zigzag braid Page 81

Star knot Page 72

Turk's head braid Page 77

Three-strand plait Page 82

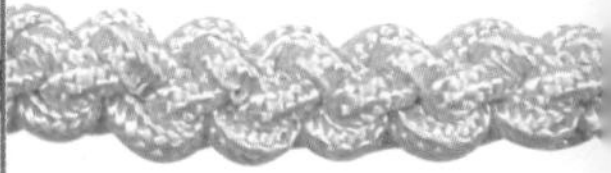

Phoenix tail knot Page 86

Footrope knot Page 69

Planet Earth knot Page 73

Blimp knot Page 78

Four-strand plait Page 83

Ring hitching Page 87

Matthew Walker knot Page 70

Uranus knot Page 74

Braid knot Page 79

Four-strand braid Page 84

Spanish hitching Page 88

Flat Turk's head knot Page 75

Double chain Page 80

Six-strand plait Page 85

Eight-plait grommet Page 89

Horizontal figure-of-eight chain
Page 93

Round mat Page 97

Triangular knot Page 101

Trefoil knot Page 90

Carrick mat Page 94

Eight-strand square knot Page 98

Heart knot Page 102

Single-strand star knot Page 91

Oval mat Page 95

Celtic cross Page 99

Celtic square knot Page 104

Plum blossom knot Page 105

Figure-of-eight chain Page 92

Prolong knot Page 96

Circle of life Page 100

Guinevere knot Page 106

Snake knot

In China, a snake is considered as a bringer of good fortune as well as a guarder of treasure. Perhaps use this knot to make a necklace for a treasured pendant. This knot also looks really pretty when tied using two different-colored cords.

Chinese knots have been used for centuries as decorations, and many of them are considered to enhance luck, prosperity, health, or protection against evil. Japanese knots are often ceremonial parts of clothing.

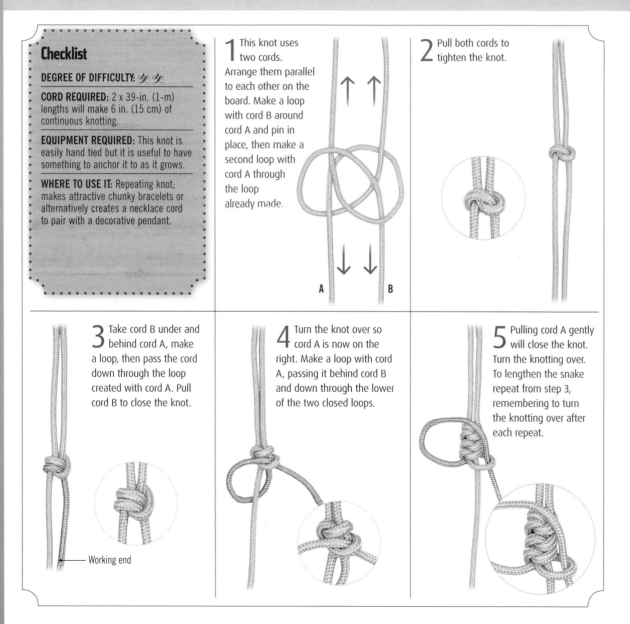

Checklist

DEGREE OF DIFFICULTY: ✍ ✍

CORD REQUIRED: 2 x 39-in. (1-m) lengths will make 6 in. (15 cm) of continuous knotting.

EQUIPMENT REQUIRED: This knot is easily hand tied but it is useful to have something to anchor it to as it grows.

WHERE TO USE IT: Repeating knot; makes attractive chunky bracelets or alternatively creates a necklace cord to pair with a decorative pendant.

1 This knot uses two cords. Arrange them parallel to each other on the board. Make a loop with cord B around cord A and pin in place, then make a second loop with cord A through the loop already made.

A   B

2 Pull both cords to tighten the knot.

3 Take cord B under and behind cord A, make a loop, then pass the cord down through the loop created with cord A. Pull cord B to close the knot.

Working end

4 Turn the knot over so cord A is now on the right. Make a loop with cord A, passing it behind cord B and down through the lower of the two closed loops.

5 Pulling cord A gently will close the knot. Turn the knotting over. To lengthen the snake repeat from step 3, remembering to turn the knotting over after each repeat.

Firecracker knot

If tails are left when tying the firecracker knot, a pretty tassel is created. This looks particularly nice on a pair of dangly earrings. In China, firecrackers are thought to frighten away evil spirits and firecracker knots are often used in symbolic wall hangings.

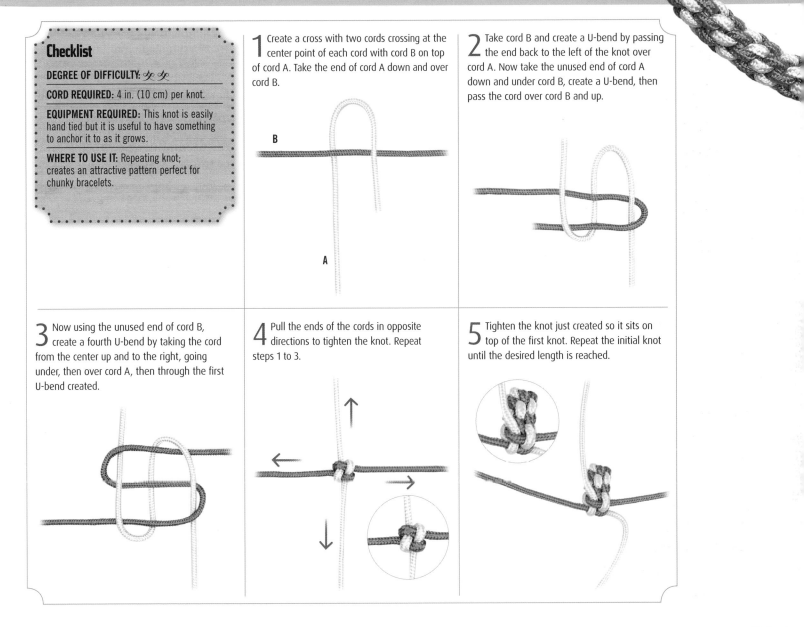

Checklist

DEGREE OF DIFFICULTY: ✂ ✂

CORD REQUIRED: 4 in. (10 cm) per knot.

EQUIPMENT REQUIRED: This knot is easily hand tied but it is useful to have something to anchor it to as it grows.

WHERE TO USE IT: Repeating knot; creates an attractive pattern perfect for chunky bracelets.

1 Create a cross with two cords crossing at the center point of each cord with cord B on top of cord A. Take the end of cord A down and over cord B.

2 Take cord B and create a U-bend by passing the end back to the left of the knot over cord A. Now take the unused end of cord A down and under cord B, create a U-bend, then pass the cord over cord B and up.

3 Now using the unused end of cord B, create a fourth U-bend by taking the cord from the center up and to the right, going under, then over cord A, then through the first U-bend created.

4 Pull the ends of the cords in opposite directions to tighten the knot. Repeat steps 1 to 3.

5 Tighten the knot just created so it sits on top of the first knot. Repeat the initial knot until the desired length is reached.

Button knot

Button knots are incredibly versatile and can be used in a wide range of projects. Traditionally, these round knots were actually used as buttons, hence their name. Button knots can be tied with one cord—if it is tied with two cords it is called a double button knot.

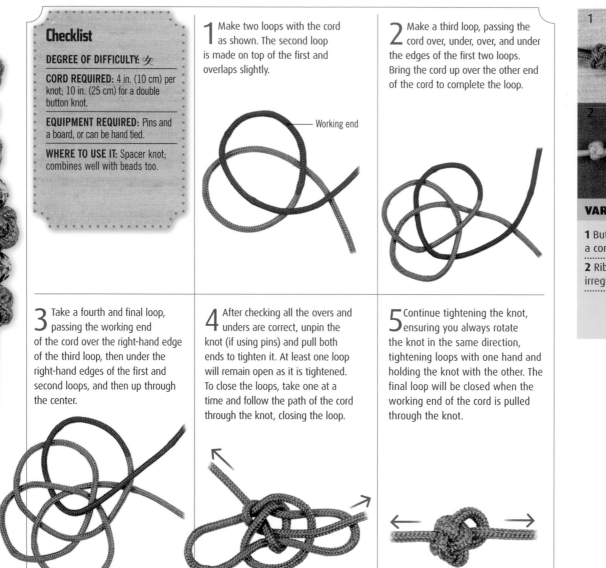

Checklist

DEGREE OF DIFFICULTY: ✂

CORD REQUIRED: 4 in. (10 cm) per knot; 10 in. (25 cm) for a double button knot.

EQUIPMENT REQUIRED: Pins and a board, or can be hand tied.

WHERE TO USE IT: Spacer knot; combines well with beads too.

1 Make two loops with the cord as shown. The second loop is made on top of the first and overlaps slightly.

Working end

2 Make a third loop, passing the cord over, under, over, and under the edges of the first two loops. Bring the cord up over the other end of the cord to complete the loop.

3 Take a fourth and final loop, passing the working end of the cord over the right-hand edge of the third loop, then under the right-hand edges of the first and second loops, and then up through the center.

4 After checking all the overs and unders are correct, unpin the knot (if using pins) and pull both ends to tighten it. At least one loop will remain open as it is tightened. To close the loops, take one at a time and follow the path of the cord through the knot, closing the loop.

5 Continue tightening the knot, ensuring you always rotate the knot in the same direction, tightening loops with one hand and holding the knot with the other. The final loop will be closed when the working end of the cord is pulled through the knot.

VARIATIONS

1 Button knots tied around a cord.

2 Ribbon cord creates an irregular look.

Pineapple knot

The Pineapple knot is an extended button knot (see opposite) and is easier to tie if you can already tie a button knot. It is also known as an extended diamond knot.

Checklist

DEGREE OF DIFFICULTY: 🧵 🧵 🧵

CORD REQUIRED: 8 in. (20 cm) per knot.

EQUIPMENT REQUIRED: Pins and a board.

WHERE TO USE IT: Spacer knot; looks particularly nice with chunky beads.

1 This knot is started in the middle of the cord and is tied with both ends. Take both ends of the cord up and over the front of the cord, making two open loops, with end A going over the bottom of end B, and end B passing over end A at the top.

2 Take end A up and down and round to the right, passing over end B, over itself, under end B, then up to close the loop. Repeat the process with end B, following the overs and unders shown to complete a loop at the bottom of the knot.

Working end →

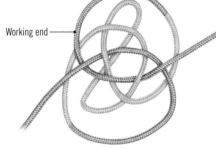

3 Take end A back to the left of the knot, passing through the loop at the top, and pull the cord gently to tighten the loop. Take end B from left to right, through the loop at the bottom, then pull through.

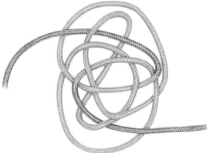

4 Take end B up and round into a large loop, then pass it through the middle of the knotting, under all the cords until coming up at the center, then down to the bottom of the knot over the rest of the cords. Take end A down and up to create a large loop at the bottom. Pass the end up under the cords, then out at the center, then down over the cords to join end B.

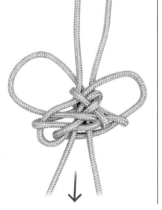

5 Hold the cord at the middle point with one hand and the two cord ends with the other hand. Pull your hands apart to begin to tighten the knot.

6 To tighten the knot, start with the largest loop and follow the path of the cord through the knot until you reach the end and pull the cord to close the loop. Each end of the cord is tightened separately and the cord needs to be followed up and down as well as around the knot.

Sliding button knot

The sliding button knot is another variation of the very versatile button knot (see page 30) and involves tying the knot around a cord.

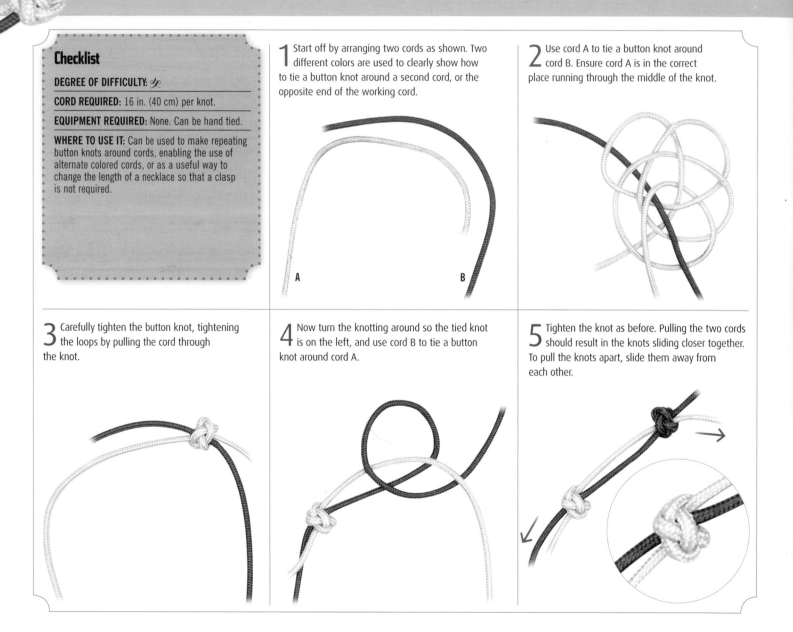

Checklist

DEGREE OF DIFFICULTY: ✂

CORD REQUIRED: 16 in. (40 cm) per knot.

EQUIPMENT REQUIRED: None. Can be hand tied.

WHERE TO USE IT: Can be used to make repeating button knots around cords, enabling the use of alternate colored cords, or as a useful way to change the length of a necklace so that a clasp is not required.

1 Start off by arranging two cords as shown. Two different colors are used to clearly show how to tie a button knot around a second cord, or the opposite end of the working cord.

A   B

2 Use cord A to tie a button knot around cord B. Ensure cord A is in the correct place running through the middle of the knot.

3 Carefully tighten the button knot, tightening the loops by pulling the cord through the knot.

4 Now turn the knotting around so the tied knot is on the left, and use cord B to tie a button knot around cord A.

5 Tighten the knot as before. Pulling the two cords should result in the knots sliding closer together. To pull the knots apart, slide them away from each other.

Double flat button knot

This is another variation of the button knot and can be tied with one cord or doubled as it is here. A stitch may be required on the back of the knot to keep it stable.

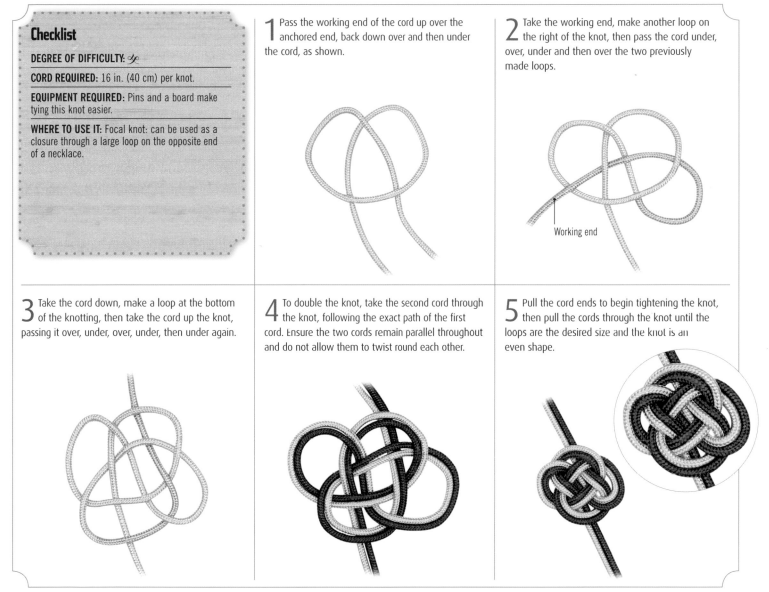

Checklist

DEGREE OF DIFFICULTY: ✂

CORD REQUIRED: 16 in. (40 cm) per knot.

EQUIPMENT REQUIRED: Pins and a board make tying this knot easier.

WHERE TO USE IT: Focal knot: can be used as a closure through a large loop on the opposite end of a necklace.

1 Pass the working end of the cord up over the anchored end, back down over and then under the cord, as shown.

2 Take the working end, make another loop on the right of the knot, then pass the cord under, over, under and then over the two previously made loops.

Working end

3 Take the cord down, make a loop at the bottom of the knotting, then take the cord up the knot, passing it over, under, over, under, then under again.

4 To double the knot, take the second cord through the knot, following the exact path of the first cord. Ensure the two cords remain parallel throughout and do not allow them to twist round each other.

5 Pull the cord ends to begin tightening the knot, then pull the cords through the knot until the loops are the desired size and the knot is an even shape.

Double coin knot

In China, this knot represents long life and prosperity as its shape represents two overlapping coins. The knot can be tied in sequence with one cord end or two to create two different effects.

Checklist

DEGREE OF DIFFICULTY:

CORD REQUIRED: 10 in. (25 cm) per knot.

EQUIPMENT REQUIRED: None. Can be hand tied.

WHERE TO USE IT: Tied in sequence to make wide necklaces or bracelets.

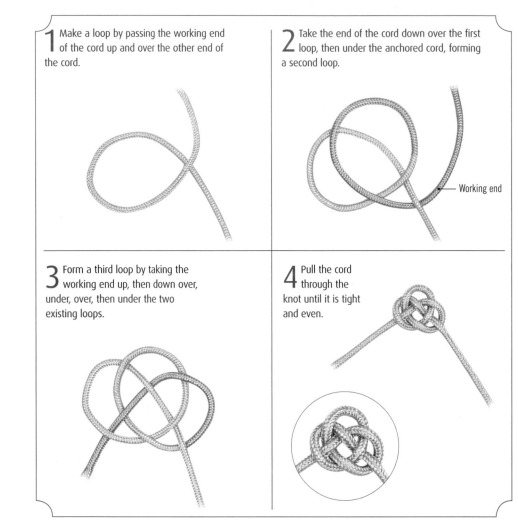

1 Make a loop by passing the working end of the cord up and over the other end of the cord.

2 Take the end of the cord down over the first loop, then under the anchored cord, forming a second loop.

— Working end

3 Form a third loop by taking the working end up, then down over, under, over, then under the two existing loops.

4 Pull the cord through the knot until it is tight and even.

VARIATIONS

1 Large bead on middle loop.

2 Silk and lurex tied side by side.

Double connection knot

This knot is a very simple knot that is useful for gathering two cords together. They can be tied in sequence, which creates an attractive crossover effect. This knot looks better tied with two different color cords.

Checklist

DEGREE OF DIFFICULTY: 🏃

CORD REQUIRED: 3 in. (7 cm) per knot.

EQUIPMENT REQUIRED: None. Can be hand tied.

WHERE TO USE IT: Spacer knot; looks pretty with beads.

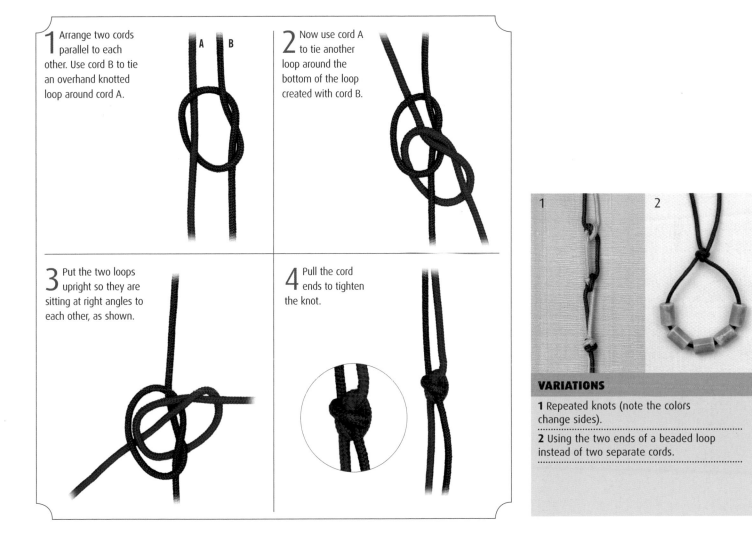

1 Arrange two cords parallel to each other. Use cord B to tie an overhand knotted loop around cord A.

2 Now use cord A to tie another loop around the bottom of the loop created with cord B.

3 Put the two loops upright so they are sitting at right angles to each other, as shown.

4 Pull the cord ends to tighten the knot.

VARIATIONS

1 Repeated knots (note the colors change sides).

2 Using the two ends of a beaded loop instead of two separate cords.

Cross knot

This knot is a nice, stable knot that is easy to tie. It can be tied with one cord or two, and if tied with two cords it looks best done with two different colors. In Chinese the cross means ten.

Checklist

DEGREE OF DIFFICULTY:

CORD REQUIRED: 10 in. (25 cm) per knot.

EQUIPMENT REQUIRED: This knot can be hand tied though a board is useful when tying the knot for the first time.

WHERE TO USE IT: Spacer knot; makes an attractive repeating pattern.

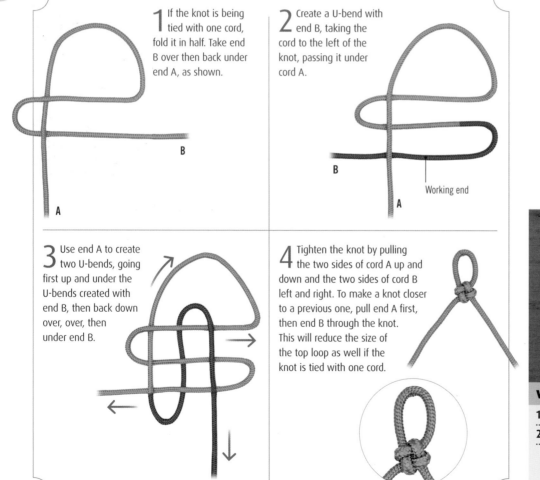

1 If the knot is being tied with one cord, fold it in half. Take end B over then back under end A, as shown.

2 Create a U-bend with end B, taking the cord to the left of the knot, passing it under cord A.

Working end

3 Use end A to create two U-bends, going first up and under the U-bends created with end B, then back down over, over, then under end B.

4 Tighten the knot by pulling the two sides of cord A up and down and the two sides of cord B left and right. To make a knot closer to a previous one, pull end A first, then end B through the knot. This will reduce the size of the top loop as well if the knot is tied with one cord.

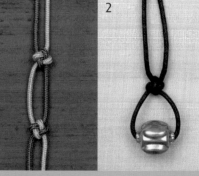

VARIATIONS

1 Using two different color cords.

2 Single cord with large bead on the loop.

Prosperity knot

This knot has the appearance of a sequence of double coin knots (see page 34), which is why it is called a prosperity knot. If you use this knot with a pendant, the pendant needs to be threaded to the middle of the cord before tying the knot.

Checklist

DEGREE OF DIFFICULTY: ✂ ✂

CORD REQUIRED: 16 in. (40 cm) per knot.

EQUIPMENT REQUIRED: Pins and a board.

WHERE TO USE IT: Focal knot; can be used with or without a pendant.

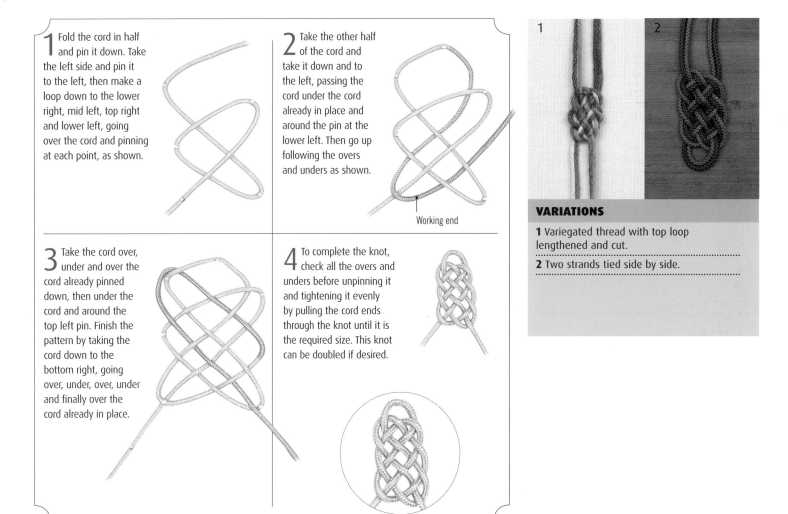

1 Fold the cord in half and pin it down. Take the left side and pin it to the left, then make a loop down to the lower right, mid left, top right and lower left, going over the cord and pinning at each point, as shown.

2 Take the other half of the cord and take it down and to the left, passing the cord under the cord already in place and around the pin at the lower left. Then go up following the overs and unders as shown.

Working end

3 Take the cord over, under and over the cord already pinned down, then under the cord and around the top left pin. Finish the pattern by taking the cord down to the bottom right, going over, under, over, under and finally over the cord already in place.

4 To complete the knot, check all the overs and unders before unpinning it and tightening it evenly by pulling the cord ends through the knot until it is the required size. This knot can be doubled if desired.

VARIATIONS

1 Variegated thread with top loop lengthened and cut.

2 Two strands tied side by side.

Pipa knot

This knot makes an ideal shape for earrings and its shape also gives rise to the pipa knot's alternative name, the teardrop knot. It's called pipa because it is of a similar shape to a Chinese string instrument called a pipa.

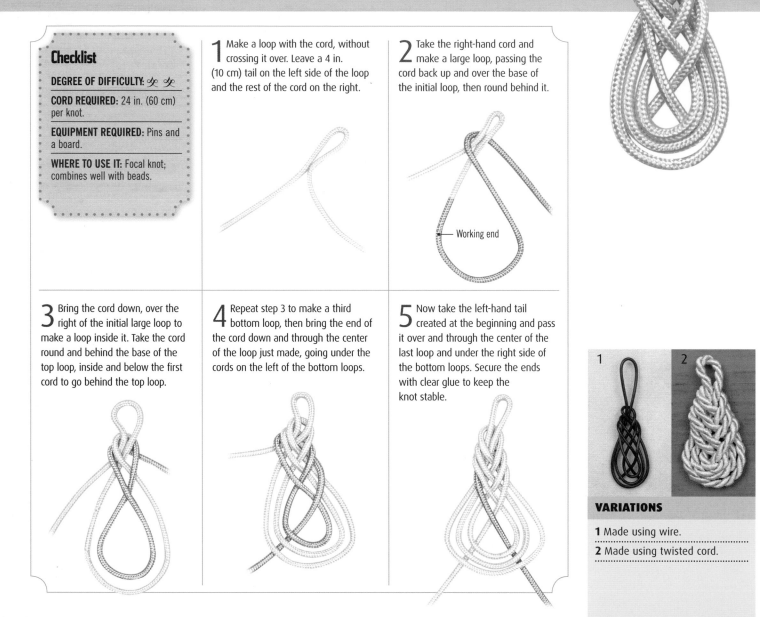

Checklist

DEGREE OF DIFFICULTY: ✂ ✂

CORD REQUIRED: 24 in. (60 cm) per knot.

EQUIPMENT REQUIRED: Pins and a board.

WHERE TO USE IT: Focal knot; combines well with beads.

1 Make a loop with the cord, without crossing it over. Leave a 4 in. (10 cm) tail on the left side of the loop and the rest of the cord on the right.

2 Take the right-hand cord and make a large loop, passing the cord back up and over the base of the initial loop, then round behind it.

Working end

3 Bring the cord down, over the right of the initial large loop to make a loop inside it. Take the cord round and behind the base of the top loop, inside and below the first cord to go behind the top loop.

4 Repeat step 3 to make a third bottom loop, then bring the end of the cord down and through the center of the loop just made, going under the cords on the left of the bottom loops.

5 Now take the left-hand tail created at the beginning and pass it over and through the center of the last loop and under the right side of the bottom loops. Secure the ends with clear glue to keep the knot stable.

VARIATIONS

1 Made using wire.

2 Made using twisted cord.

Plafond knot

This knot looks complicated to tie but it is worth persevering with. Tighten it slowly. It is called the plafond knot due to its similarity to ceiling centers in Chinese temples ("plafond" is French for ceiling). This knot is also referred to as the Chinese lanyard knot and the spectacle knot.

Checklist

DEGREE OF DIFFICULTY: ✂ ✂ ✂

CORD REQUIRED: 28 in. (70 cm) per knot.

EQUIPMENT REQUIRED: Pins and a board.

WHERE TO USE IT: Can be tied in sequence or used as a focal knot paired with a pendant if desired.

1 Fold the cord in half, then tie four loose, large looped overhand knots (right over left and left over right). Take the left cord up and around the left of the four knots over the top loop and down through the middle of the overhand knots. Repeat with the right cord on the right side of the knot passing it under the top loop instead.

2 Take the bottom left-hand loop up to the top of the knotting at the front, and the bottom right-hand loop up at the back of the knotting but not over the loop. Flatten the knot and reduce the size of the loops by pulling the cords through the knot.

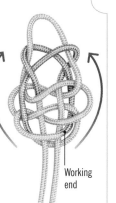

Working end

3 Take the bottom loops to the top of the knot, left one at the front, right one at the back, as before.

4 Pull the top loop and the bottom cords to tighten the knot. Pull one cord through the knot to reduce the size of the top loop to the desired size.

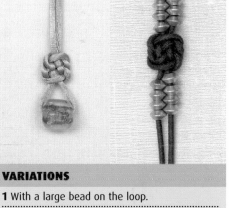

VARIATIONS

1 With a large bead on the loop.

2 Loop cut and beads added to all four ends.

Virtue knot

The pattern of the virtue knot is similar to a Buddhist motif symbolizing sun, fire, complete virtue, and power over evil. Beads can be threaded onto the cords before tying the overhand knots so the loops have beads on when the knot is tightened.

Checklist

DEGREE OF DIFFICULTY:

CORD REQUIRED: 10 in. (25 cm) per knot.

EQUIPMENT REQUIRED: Pins and a board help to keep the knotting flat.

WHERE TO USE IT: Can be tied in sequence or used as a simple focal knot.

1 Fold the cord in half and pin at the center. Make an overhand knot, leaving a loop with the left side of the cord. Make a second large looped overhand knot with the right half of the cord, going through the initial loop.

2 Pull the inside cord of both loops through the opposite overhand knot.

3 To tighten the knot pull the loops until the center closes.

4 Adjust the lengths of the loops, as required. A stitch or two will be required to prevent the knot undoing.

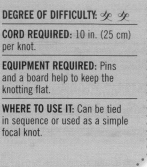

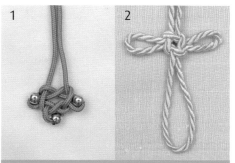

VARIATIONS

1 Loops are pulled in and held in place by the beads.

2 Twisted cord and extra-long top loop.

Clover-leaf knot

Clover leaves are considered good luck in China as they are in the West, so tie this knot for a good luck charm. It is also known as a flower knot. This knot is not the most stable so needs a stitch or two to prevent it from slipping.

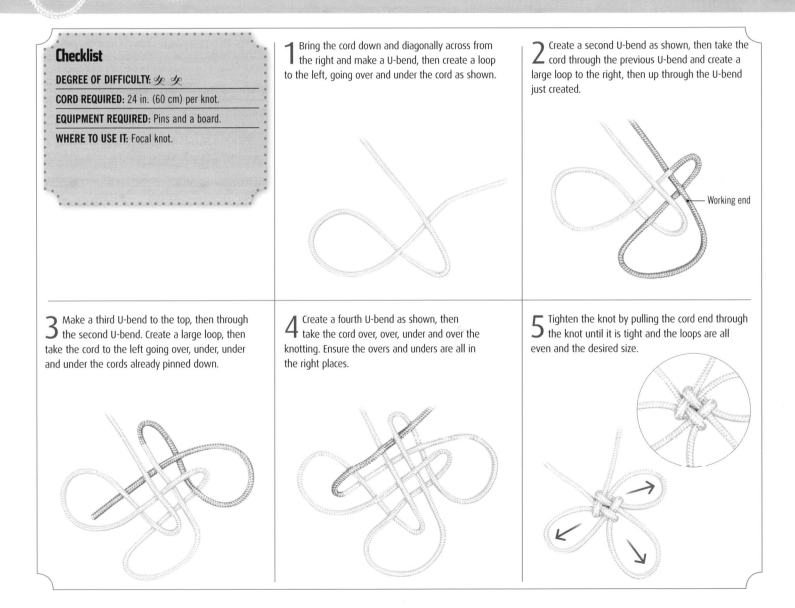

Checklist

DEGREE OF DIFFICULTY: ✎ ✎

CORD REQUIRED: 24 in. (60 cm) per knot.

EQUIPMENT REQUIRED: Pins and a board.

WHERE TO USE IT: Focal knot.

1 Bring the cord down and diagonally across from the right and make a U-bend, then create a loop to the left, going over and under the cord as shown.

2 Create a second U-bend as shown, then take the cord through the previous U-bend and create a large loop to the right, then up through the U-bend just created.

Working end

3 Make a third U-bend to the top, then through the second U-bend. Create a large loop, then take the cord to the left going over, under, under and under the cords already pinned down.

4 Create a fourth U-bend as shown, then take the cord over, over, under and over the knotting. Ensure the overs and unders are all in the right places.

5 Tighten the knot by pulling the cord end through the knot until it is tight and the loops are all even and the desired size.

Four-leaf clover knot

This knot is an extension of the clover-leaf knot (see page 41), with four leaves rather than three. Four-leaf clovers are rarer than three-leafed ones and are therefore considered luckier.

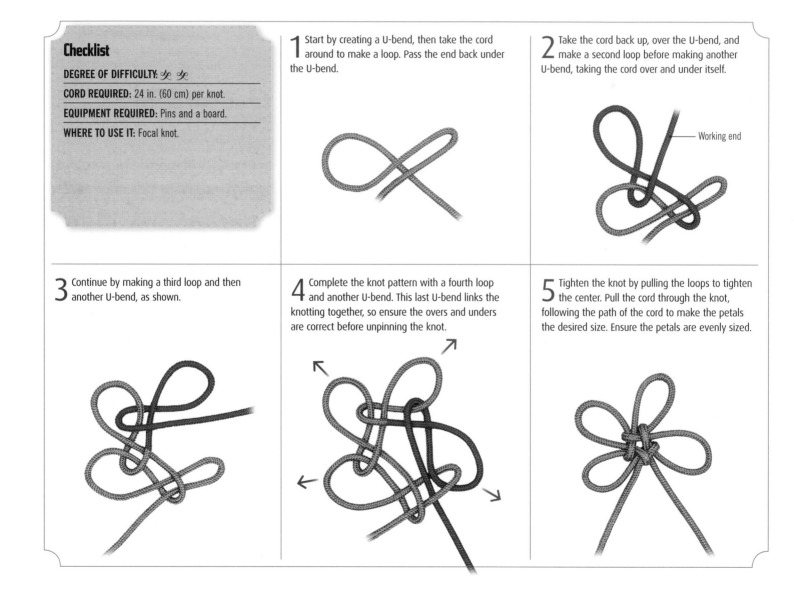

Checklist

DEGREE OF DIFFICULTY:

CORD REQUIRED: 24 in. (60 cm) per knot.

EQUIPMENT REQUIRED: Pins and a board.

WHERE TO USE IT: Focal knot.

1 Start by creating a U-bend, then take the cord around to make a loop. Pass the end back under the U-bend.

2 Take the cord back up, over the U-bend, and make a second loop before making another U-bend, taking the cord over and under itself.

Working end

3 Continue by making a third loop and then another U-bend, as shown.

4 Complete the knot pattern with a fourth loop and another U-bend. This last U-bend links the knotting together, so ensure the overs and unders are correct before unpinning the knot.

5 Tighten the knot by pulling the loops to tighten the center. Pull the cord through the knot, following the path of the cord to make the petals the desired size. Ensure the petals are evenly sized.

Chick knot

This knot is named because of its resemblance to a young bird when seen from the sky. It is made up of two knots—the mystic knot (see page 48) and the clover-leaf knot (see page 41).

(see page 48) ... (see page 41)

Checklist

DEGREE OF DIFFICULTY: ✄ ✄ ✄

CORD REQUIRED: 79 in. (2 m) per knot (or 2 x 39-in./1-m strands)

EQUIPMENT REQUIRED: Pins and a board.

WHERE TO USE IT: Use as a focal knot.

1 This knot can be tied with one or two cords. If using one, fold the cord in half and start in the middle of the cord. Create two U-bends, as shown with the right-hand side of the cord.

2 Now create the first part of the clover-leaf knot (see page 41) on the right-hand side, by creating two loops and two U-bends, as shown. Make sure all overs and unders are correct.

Working end

3 Continue the clover-leaf knot with another loop and U-bend.

4 Now take the cord back to the main body of the knot and make two U-bends as part of the mystic knot (see page 48).

5 Now take the left-hand side of the cord, or a second cord, and complete the knot pattern on the left-hand side. Follow the pattern carefully and make sure the overs and unders are all correct before unpinning the knot.

6 When tightening the knot, start with the two clover-leaf knots on either side. Reduce the sizes of the loops to the required size by pulling the cord through the knot. Reduce the size of the central mystic knot last by slowly and carefully pulling each cord though the knot, a little at a time.

Oblong knot

The oblong knot is an extension of the clover-leaf knot (see page 41), so perhaps brings extra good luck. If the loops are tightened, the knot has a distinct oblong shape. However, if you keep the loops larger, the knot creates a pretty flower shape.

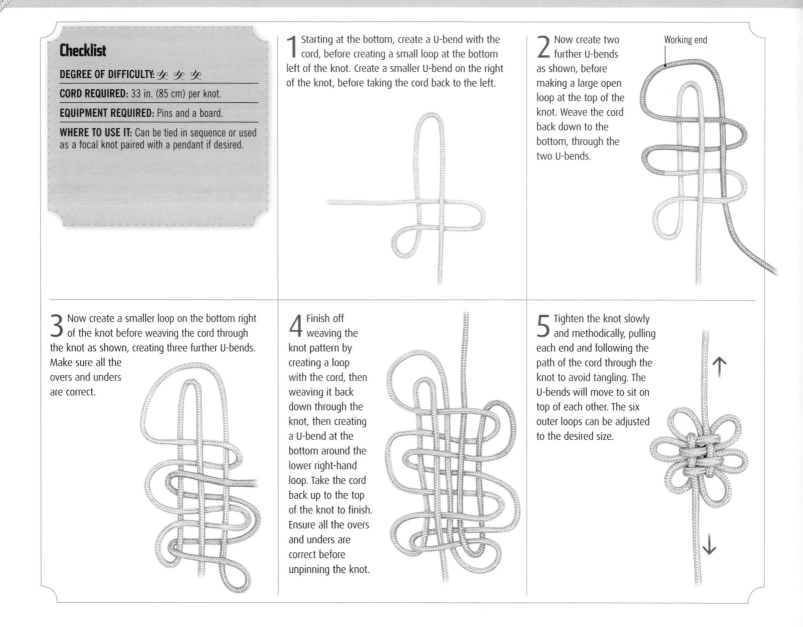

Checklist

DEGREE OF DIFFICULTY: ✸ ✸ ✸

CORD REQUIRED: 33 in. (85 cm) per knot.

EQUIPMENT REQUIRED: Pins and a board.

WHERE TO USE IT: Can be tied in sequence or used as a focal knot paired with a pendant if desired.

1 Starting at the bottom, create a U-bend with the cord, before creating a small loop at the bottom left of the knot. Create a smaller U-bend on the right of the knot, before taking the cord back to the left.

2 Now create two further U-bends as shown, before making a large open loop at the top of the knot. Weave the cord back down to the bottom, through the two U-bends.

Working end

3 Now create a smaller loop on the bottom right of the knot before weaving the cord through the knot as shown, creating three further U-bends. Make sure all the overs and unders are correct.

4 Finish off weaving the knot pattern by creating a loop with the cord, then weaving it back down through the knot, then creating a U-bend at the bottom around the lower right-hand loop. Take the cord back up to the top of the knot to finish. Ensure all the overs and unders are correct before unpinning the knot.

5 Tighten the knot slowly and methodically, pulling each end and following the path of the cord through the knot to avoid tangling. The U-bends will move to sit on top of each other. The six outer loops can be adjusted to the desired size.

Good luck knot

This knot is also thought of as a bringer of good luck. Chinese knot jewelry makes a great gift, as it brings good luck to both the recipient and the giver. This knot looks impressive but is actually fairly simple to tie.

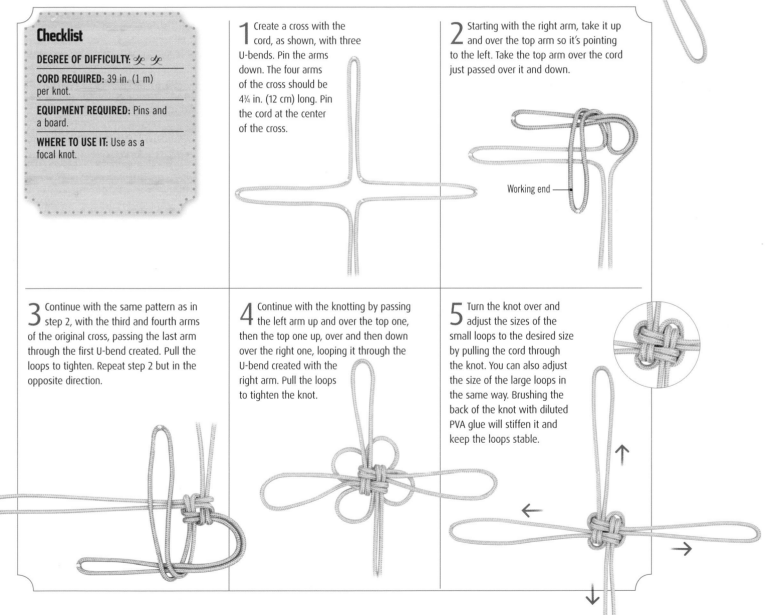

Checklist

DEGREE OF DIFFICULTY: ✂ ✂

CORD REQUIRED: 39 in. (1 m) per knot.

EQUIPMENT REQUIRED: Pins and a board.

WHERE TO USE IT: Use as a focal knot.

1 Create a cross with the cord, as shown, with three U-bends. Pin the arms down. The four arms of the cross should be 4¾ in. (12 cm) long. Pin the cord at the center of the cross.

2 Starting with the right arm, take it up and over the top arm so it's pointing to the left. Take the top arm over the cord just passed over it and down.

Working end

3 Continue with the same pattern as in step 2, with the third and fourth arms of the original cross, passing the last arm through the first U-bend created. Pull the loops to tighten. Repeat step 2 but in the opposite direction.

4 Continue with the knotting by passing the left arm up and over the top one, then the top one up, over and then down over the right one, looping it through the U-bend created with the right arm. Pull the loops to tighten the knot.

5 Turn the knot over and adjust the sizes of the small loops to the desired size by pulling the cord through the knot. You can also adjust the size of the large loops in the same way. Brushing the back of the knot with diluted PVA glue will stiffen it and keep the loops stable.

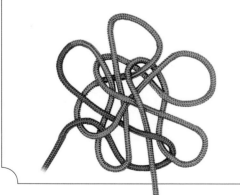

Round brocade knot

This knot is a very attractive focal knot. Keep the loops large for using as a pendant on a necklace or make them smaller for a more compact knot that makes pretty earrings.

Checklist

DEGREE OF DIFFICULTY: ✄ ✄ ✄

CORD REQUIRED: 36 in. (90 cm) per knot.

EQUIPMENT REQUIRED: Pins and a board.

WHERE TO USE IT: Focal knot; looks good with a pendant.

1 Fold the cord in half and anchor it at the halfway point. Create two loops as shown, by taking end B around and under end A, then over end A after creating the second loop. When tying the knot keep the loops the same size.

2 Now create a further loop on the right-hand side and pass the cord to the left of the knot, under, under and over the knotting, then back over the cord to create another loop on the right of the knot. Take the cord up under the knotting through the top loop and back down to the bottom of the knot.

Working end

3 Now take end A up, under and through the small loop at the top of the left of the knot, creating a loop at the bottom left side of the knot.

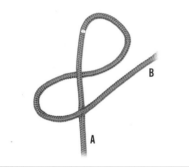

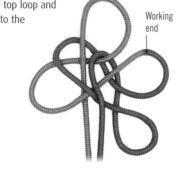

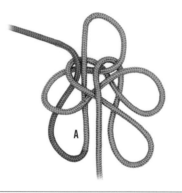

4 Create a large loop at the top of the left side of the knot, then take the cord down and to the right side of the knot, carefully following the overs and unders as shown. Take the cord through the bottom right loop then back to the left of the knot, going under, under, under, then over the cords, as shown.

5 Make a large loop on the right side, then take the cord through to the left of the knot, going through the middle right loop, under the bottom right loop, then back to the left side of the knot. Ensure all the overs and unders are correct before unpinning the knot.

6 Close the knot by pulling the loops evenly outward. The loops should be evenly sized but can be made smaller if desired by pulling the cords through the knot, following the pattern made when tying the knot.

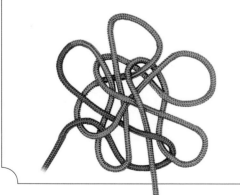

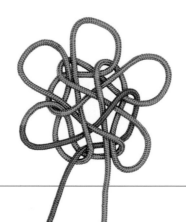

Pectoral knot

This triangular knot tightens similar to the mystic knot (see page 48), making a surprisingly compact knot for the space the knot pattern takes up when tying. It looks nice with a pendant attached to the bottom on a necklace.

Checklist

DEGREE OF DIFFICULTY: ✗ ✗ ✗

CORD REQUIRED: 45 in. (1.15 m) per knot.

EQUIPMENT REQUIRED: Pins and a board.

WHERE TO USE IT: Use as a focal knot paired with a pendant.

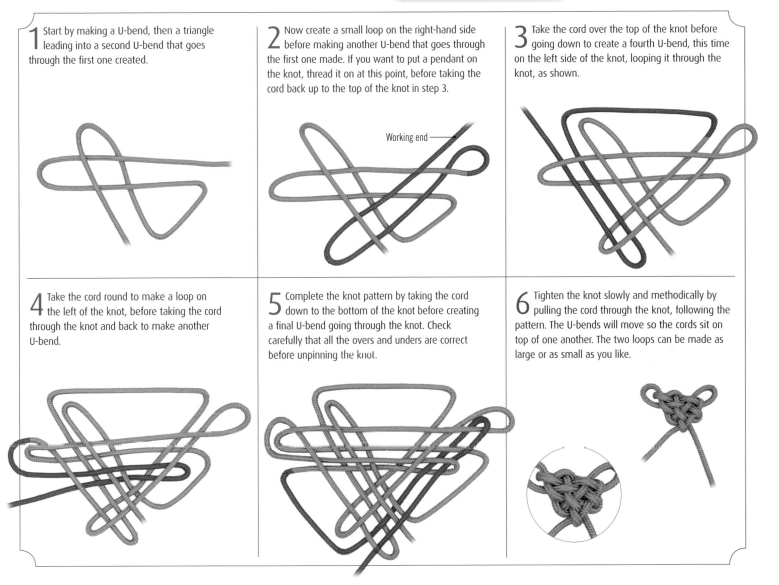

1 Start by making a U-bend, then a triangle leading into a second U-bend that goes through the first one created.

2 Now create a small loop on the right-hand side before making another U-bend that goes through the first one made. If you want to put a pendant on the knot, thread it on at this point, before taking the cord back up to the top of the knot in step 3.

Working end —

3 Take the cord over the top of the knot before going down to create a fourth U-bend, this time on the left side of the knot, looping it through the knot, as shown.

4 Take the cord round to make a loop on the left of the knot, before taking the cord through the knot and back to make another U-bend.

5 Complete the knot pattern by taking the cord down to the bottom of the knot before creating a final U-bend going through the knot. Check carefully that all the overs and unders are correct before unpinning the knot.

6 Tighten the knot slowly and methodically by pulling the cord through the knot, following the pattern. The U-bends will move so the cords sit on top of one another. The two loops can be made as large or as small as you like.

Mystic knot

The mystic knot is also known as a pan chang knot, which means "endless." This knot represents the Chinese buddhist belief that life exists forever. It is not possible to tie this knot in the hand—a board and pins are required. It can be tied with one or two cords (with two cords only six loops are created).

Checklist

DEGREE OF DIFFICULTY: ✂ ✂ ✂

CORD REQUIRED: 60 in. (1.5 m).

EQUIPMENT REQUIRED: Pins and a board.

WHERE TO USE IT: Use as a focal knot on a necklace or earrings, or combined with a pendant bead.

1 Find the center of the cord and secure it with a pin in the top left-hand corner of the board. Use the right-hand half of the cord to create two vertical loops, then the left-hand half to create two horizontal loops as shown, checking all the overs and unders are correct.

2 Now use the left-hand half of the cord to create two more vertical loops, checking the overs and unders.

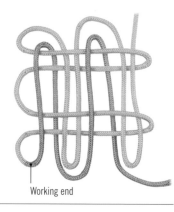

Working end

3 Make two more vertical loops using the left-hand cord to complete tying the knot. Check all the overs and unders are in the correct places before carefully unpinning the knot from the board.

4 Pull the outer seven loops to start tightening the knot. To get the best results pull the loops evenly and all at the same time. The cords in the center will move to sit on top of each other where they were side by side, doubling the thickness of the center of the knot.

5 To tidy up the knot and reduce the size of the loops, start at the point that was the center of the cord. Pull the cord through the knot, carefully following its course and reducing the loops to the required size. The loops can be left at any size but should be even.

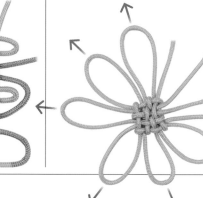

VARIATIONS

1 Shiny, variegated cord.
2 Tied with two colors.

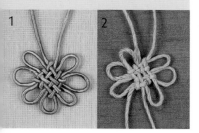

Dragonfly knot

The dragonfly knot is actually a combination of three fairly simple knots, so even though it looks quite complicated it is easily created. Beads could be combined if desired, particularly within the square knots in the body of the dragonfly.

1 You will need two cords. They do not have to be different colors but different colors create a nice effect. Lay them next to each other and tie a button knot (see page 30) with both ends together. Move the knot to the center of the cords.

2 Now tie a virtue knot, following the instructions on page 40.

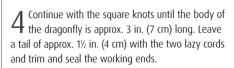

3 Tighten the virtue knot. Arrange the cords so two of the same color are on the outside of the four cords. Following the instructions on page 55, tie a square knot around the two center lazy cords.

4 Continue with the square knots until the body of the dragonfly is approx. 3 in. (7 cm) long. Leave a tail of approx. 1½ in. (4 cm) with the two lazy cords and trim and seal the working ends.

VARIATIONS

1 Using a large bead instead of the button knot.

2 Gold and silver cord button-tied with silver only and gold beads added either side of the head.

Strawberry knot

Like the dragonfly knot, the strawberry knot is made up of three different knots:
a clover-leaf knot (see page 41), the wing knot from a butterfly knot (see pages 52–53),
and a button knot (see page 30) in the center.

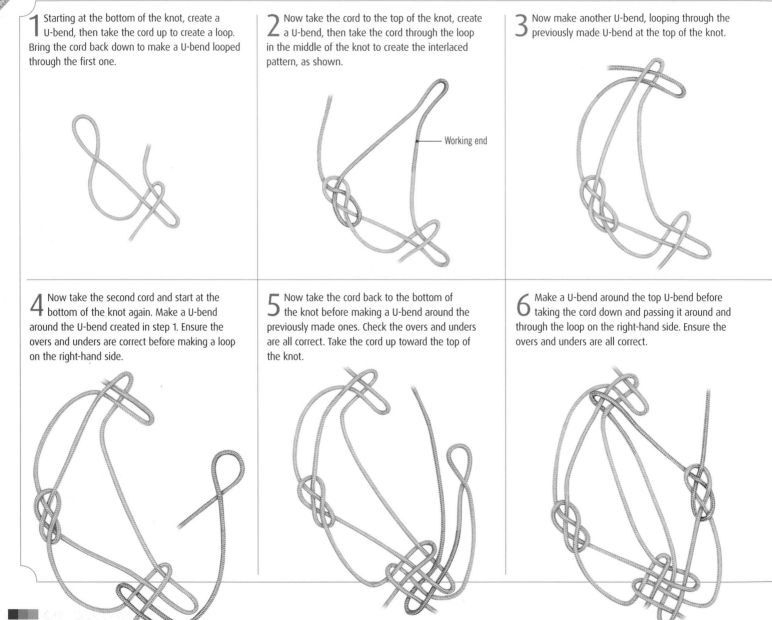

1 Starting at the bottom of the knot, create a U-bend, then take the cord up to create a loop. Bring the cord back down to make a U-bend looped through the first one.

2 Now take the cord to the top of the knot, create a U-bend, then take the cord through the loop in the middle of the knot to create the interlaced pattern, as shown.

— Working end

3 Now make another U-bend, looping through the previously made U-bend at the top of the knot.

4 Now take the second cord and start at the bottom of the knot again. Make a U-bend around the U-bend created in step 1. Ensure the overs and unders are correct before making a loop on the right-hand side.

5 Now take the cord back to the bottom of the knot before making a U-bend around the previously made ones. Check the overs and unders are all correct. Take the cord up toward the top of the knot.

6 Make a U-bend around the top U-bend before taking the cord down and passing it around and through the loop on the right-hand side. Ensure the overs and unders are all correct.

DEGREE OF DIFFICULTY: ✁ ✁ ✁

CORD REQUIRED: 47 in. (1.2 m) per knot
(or 2 x 24-in./60-cm strands), plus 6 in. (15 cm)
for the central button knot.

EQUIPMENT REQUIRED: Pins and a board.

WHERE TO USE IT: Use as a focal knot paired with
a pendant if desired.

7 Create a final U-bend at the top of the knot.
Ensure all the overs and unders in the knot are
correct before unpinning it.

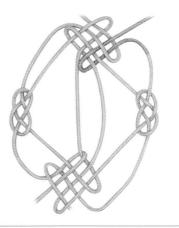

8 Start tightening the knot by tightening the
two clover-leaf knots at the top and bottom
and the two butterfly wing knots. Keep a careful
hold of all the cords to ensure they don't become
unraveled. You will end up with two long strands in
the middle of the knot.

9 With a third cord, tie a button knot around the
two middle cords, following the instructions for
tying a sliding button knot (see page 32). Trim and
seal the ends of this cord.

10 Now tighten the knot. This is a slow
process and is made easier with two
different-colored cords. Each cord will need to be
pulled through the knot one at a time, exactly
following the knot pattern. Work slowly and
methodically.

VARIATIONS

1 Two colors with a bead wired into the
middle instead of the button knot.

2 The first two cords are the same color,
the third cord different.

Butterfly knot

This knot is not the easiest to tie but is worth the effort. It can be tied with two different-colored cords, which can make tying simpler, particularly if you are new to knot-tying. Butterfly knots are symbols of joy, summer, longevity, and conjugal bliss.

1 This knot can be tied with one or two cords. It is tied in two halves. If using one cord, fold it in half and pin the middle. Starting with the right-hand side, create two U-bends, as shown.

2 Now take the cord up and create a loop before coming back down to make a U-bend around the two bends already created.

Working end

3 Now create a modified figure-of-eight shape as shown, going through the loop made in step 2. This creates the pattern on the butterfly's wing.

4 Now make a large loop before taking the cord back through the knot to create another U-bend around the first two. This completes the right side of the butterfly.

5 Now take the other cord and create a U-bend as shown, making sure the cord goes over and under the previous cords in the correct places.

6 Create a second U-bend through the knot with the left-hand end of the new cord.

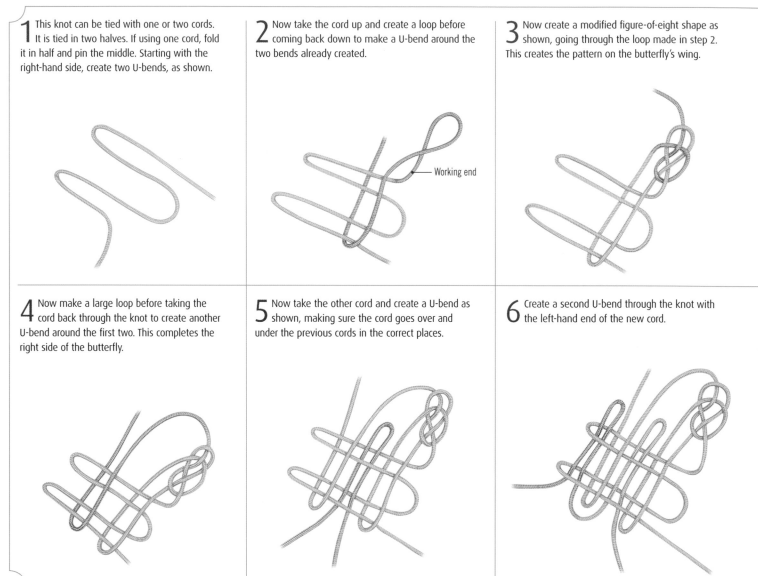

Checklist

DEGREE OF DIFFICULTY: ✄ ✄ ✄

CORD REQUIRED: 79 in. (2 m) per knot (or 2 x 39-in./1-m strands).

EQUIPMENT REQUIRED: Pins and a board.

WHERE TO USE IT: Use as a focal knot.

7 Make a loop on the left-hand side before taking the cord back through the knot to make another U-bend.

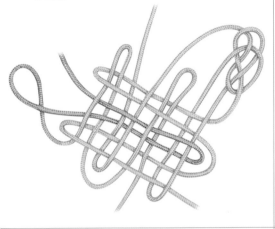

8 Create the wing pattern on the left side by making another modified figure-of-eight, as shown.

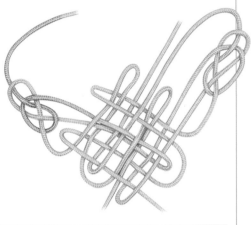

9 Now create the left-hand wing by making a large loop before taking the cord through the knot to make a final U-bend. Ensure all the overs and unders are correct before unpinning the knot.

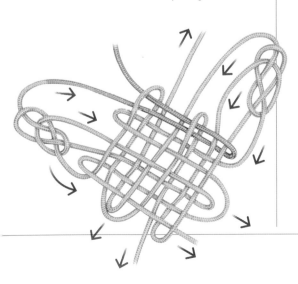

10 Tighten the knot by slowly pulling the cords through the knot, doing one side at a time. Make sure the butterfly's wings are the same size.

VARIATIONS

1 Two colors of cord.

2 With beads on the top wings.

Many of the Western knots are basic macramé, which was traditionally used for bags and home decor items, but is now more commonly seen in jewelry. Others are from Celtic heritage.

Half knot

This knot is a macramé knot. It is the first half of the square knot (see opposite). Tied repeatedly in a chain, it creates an attractive twisting effect. Approximately eight knots are required to create a complete twist.

Checklist

DEGREE OF DIFFICULTY:

CORD REQUIRED: 16 in. (40 cm) (folded in half) per 10 knots.

EQUIPMENT REQUIRED: Can be hand tied but it is useful to anchor the cord.

WHERE TO USE IT: Repeating knot; makes attractive necklace cords or simple bracelets.

1 Fold the two cords in half and arrange them parallel to each other. The two middle cords will be the lazy cords (L) that the knots will be tied around.

2 Pass the left-hand cord over the two lazy cords.

Working end

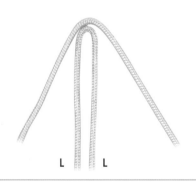

L   L

3 Now take the right-hand cord over the left-hand cord, over the two lazy cords and through the loop created on the left-hand side. Pull the cord ends to tighten.

4 Repeat steps 2 and 3 until the knotting is the desired length. The tighter these knots are tied, the more attractive the pattern will be.

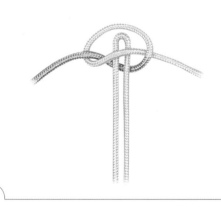

Square knot

The square knot is a macramé knot, also known as a reef knot or flat knot. Square knots are tied with two cords working around any number of lazy cords (usually two). They can be tied with interchanging lazy and working cords or in columns.

1 Arrange the cords so that the two working cords are on the outside and the lazy cords (L) are in the center (use as many lazy cords as you like to make the rope thicker). Take the left-hand working cord over the lazy cords and underneath the right-hand working cord.

2 Take the right-hand working cord under the lazy cords and up through the loop created on the left-hand side. Pull the two working cords to tighten the knot. This will finish the first half of the square knot.

3 Take the right-hand working cord over the lazy cords and under the left-hand working cord. Take the left-hand working cord under the lazy cords and up through the right-hand loop.

4 Pull the ends of the working cords to tighten the knot. This completes one square knot. Repeat steps 1 to 4 to complete further square knots in sequence.

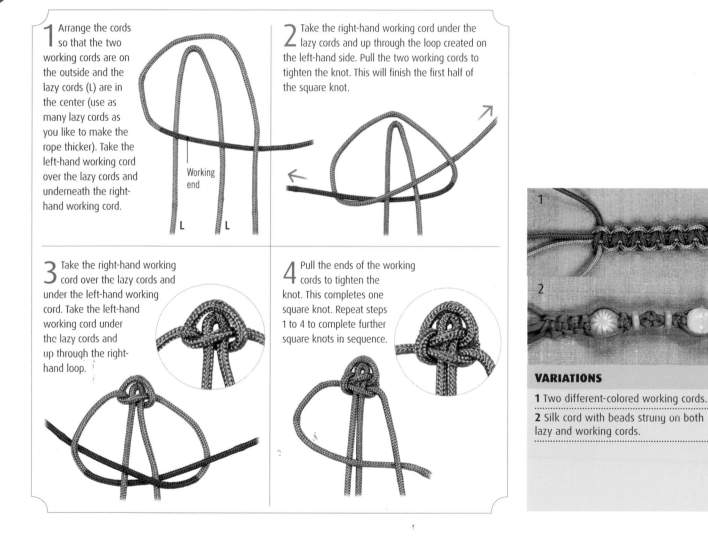

VARIATIONS

1 Two different-colored working cords.

2 Silk cord with beads strung on both lazy and working cords.

Lark's head knot

This knot is a macramé knot, traditionally used at the beginning of a macramé piece to attach the knotting to something.

Checklist

DEGREE OF DIFFICULTY:

CORD REQUIRED: 4 in. (10 cm) per knot.

EQUIPMENT REQUIRED: Something to tie the knot around, such as another cord.

WHERE TO USE IT: Anchoring knot.

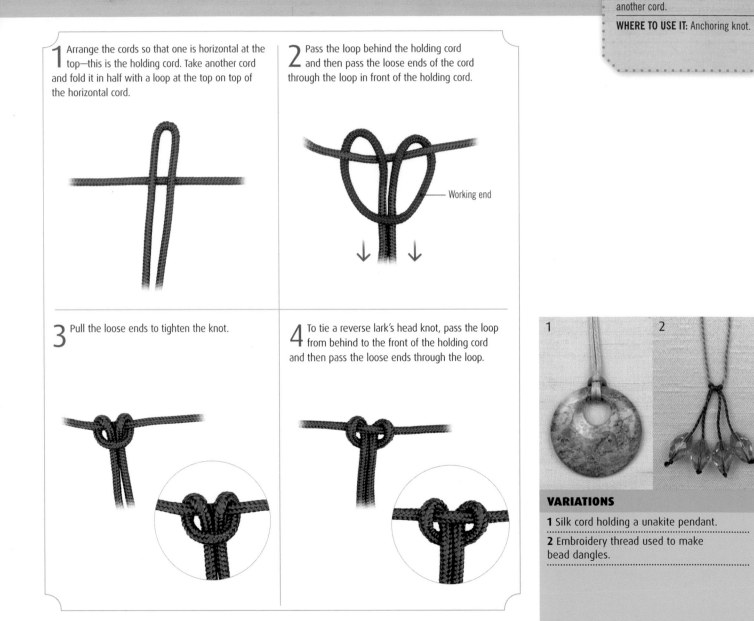

1 Arrange the cords so that one is horizontal at the top—this is the holding cord. Take another cord and fold it in half with a loop at the top on top of the horizontal cord.

2 Pass the loop behind the holding cord and then pass the loose ends of the cord through the loop in front of the holding cord.

Working end

3 Pull the loose ends to tighten the knot.

4 To tie a reverse lark's head knot, pass the loop from behind to the front of the holding cord and then pass the loose ends through the loop.

VARIATIONS

1 Silk cord holding a unakite pendant.

2 Embroidery thread used to make bead dangles.

Vertical lark's head knot

This is a variation of the lark's head knot (see opposite). This variation allows a chain of lark's head knots to be created. Using different-colored cords for the two pairs of cords creates an interesting effect.

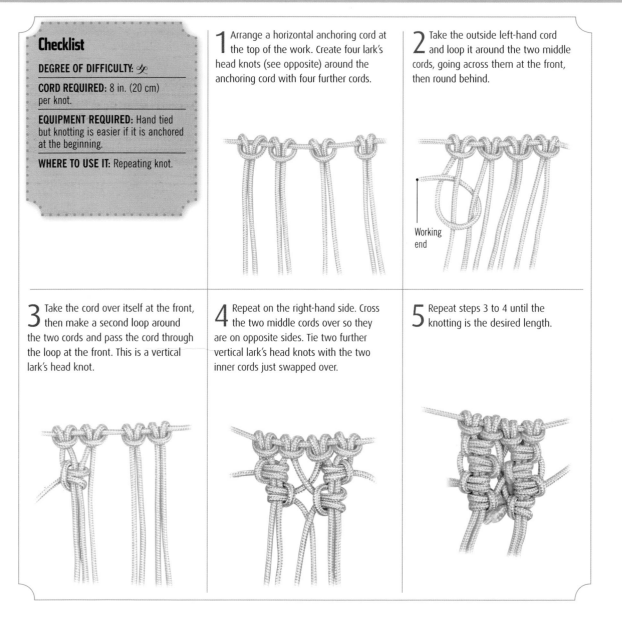

Checklist

DEGREE OF DIFFICULTY: ✂

CORD REQUIRED: 8 in. (20 cm) per knot.

EQUIPMENT REQUIRED: Hand tied but knotting is easier if it is anchored at the beginning.

WHERE TO USE IT: Repeating knot.

1 Arrange a horizontal anchoring cord at the top of the work. Create four lark's head knots (see opposite) around the anchoring cord with four further cords.

2 Take the outside left-hand cord and loop it around the two middle cords, going across them at the front, then round behind.

Working end

3 Take the cord over itself at the front, then make a second loop around the two cords and pass the cord through the loop at the front. This is a vertical lark's head knot.

4 Repeat on the right-hand side. Cross the two middle cords over so they are on opposite sides. Tie two further vertical lark's head knots with the two inner cords just swapped over.

5 Repeat steps 3 to 4 until the knotting is the desired length.

Double half hitch

This knot is a very versatile macramé knot. It can be tied vertically, horizontally, and diagonally, and also from right to left or left to right. It is also known as a clove hitch.

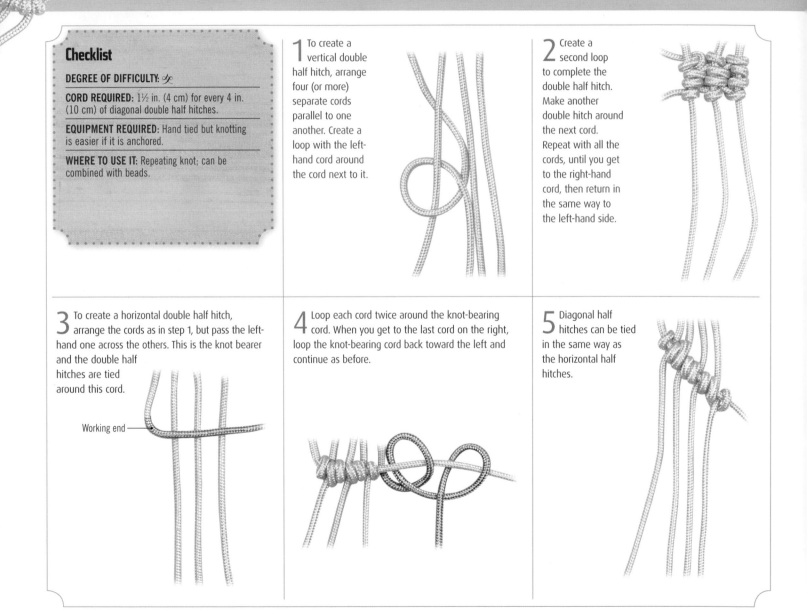

Checklist

DEGREE OF DIFFICULTY: ✂

CORD REQUIRED: 1½ in. (4 cm) for every 4 in. (10 cm) of diagonal double half hitches.

EQUIPMENT REQUIRED: Hand tied but knotting is easier if it is anchored.

WHERE TO USE IT: Repeating knot; can be combined with beads.

1 To create a vertical double half hitch, arrange four (or more) separate cords parallel to one another. Create a loop with the left-hand cord around the cord next to it.

2 Create a second loop to complete the double half hitch. Make another double hitch around the next cord. Repeat with all the cords, until you get to the right-hand cord, then return in the same way to the left-hand side.

3 To create a horizontal double half hitch, arrange the cords as in step 1, but pass the left-hand one across the others. This is the knot bearer and the double half hitches are tied around this cord.

Working end

4 Loop each cord twice around the knot-bearing cord. When you get to the last cord on the right, loop the knot-bearing cord back toward the left and continue as before.

5 Diagonal half hitches can be tied in the same way as the horizontal half hitches.

Josephine knot

This macramé knot is also known as the Chinese knot or carrick bend. It is similar to the double coin knot (see page 34), but uses two cords rather than one.

(see page 34)

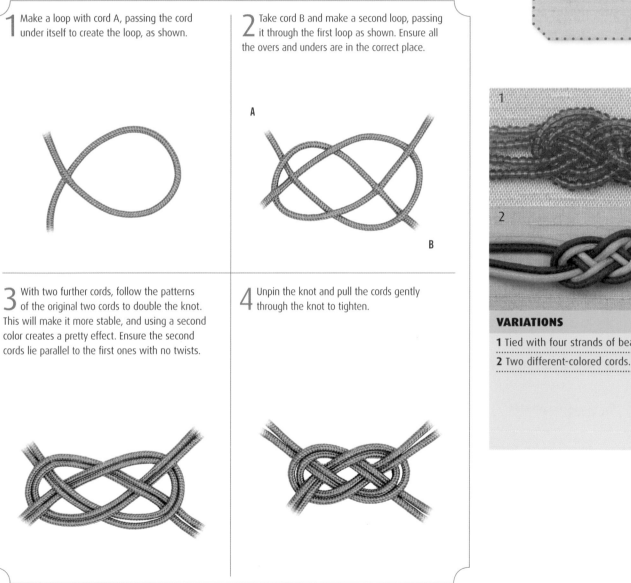

1 Make a loop with cord A, passing the cord under itself to create the loop, as shown.

2 Take cord B and make a second loop, passing it through the first loop as shown. Ensure all the overs and unders are in the correct place.

A

B

3 With two further cords, follow the patterns of the original two cords to double the knot. This will make it more stable, and using a second color creates a pretty effect. Ensure the second cords lie parallel to the first ones with no twists.

4 Unpin the knot and pull the cords gently through the knot to tighten.

1

2

VARIATIONS

1 Tied with four strands of beads.
....
2 Two different-colored cords.
....

Flat knot mat

This combination of square knots is a simple way to make a fabric of knots in any width and length.

Checklist

DEGREE OF DIFFICULTY: ✂

CORD REQUIRED: 6 in. (15 cm) per doubled cord per row.

EQUIPMENT REQUIRED: Pins and a board are helpful but not essential.

WHERE TO USE IT: Use to make wide bracelets or chokers.

1 Take a single cord and make lark's head knots (see page 56) over it with any multiple of two doubled strands (six are shown here).

2 Use each set of four cords to make a square knot (see page 55).

3 Leave the first two cords on the left loose. Use the next four strands to make a square knot and repeat to use up all the sets of cords.

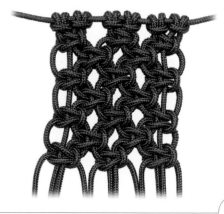

4 Starting from the left again, make another row, as in step 2. Repeat the rows until the knotting is the desired length.

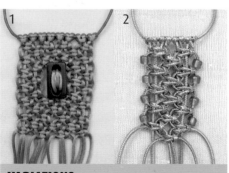

VARIATIONS

1 Wide with a big bead replacing some of the middle knots.

2 Narrow with beads on the sides.

Alpine butterfly loop

Practice this knot over a cylinder such as a narrow plastic bottle, as this leaves both hands free. When you are confident, use one or more of the fingers of your less-dominant hand.

Checklist

DEGREE OF DIFFICULTY:

CORD REQUIRED: 18 in. (45 cm) per knot.

EQUIPMENT REQUIRED: None. Can be hand tied.

WHERE TO USE IT: This is a simple looped knot that is an attractive way to attach a pendant to a simple necklace.

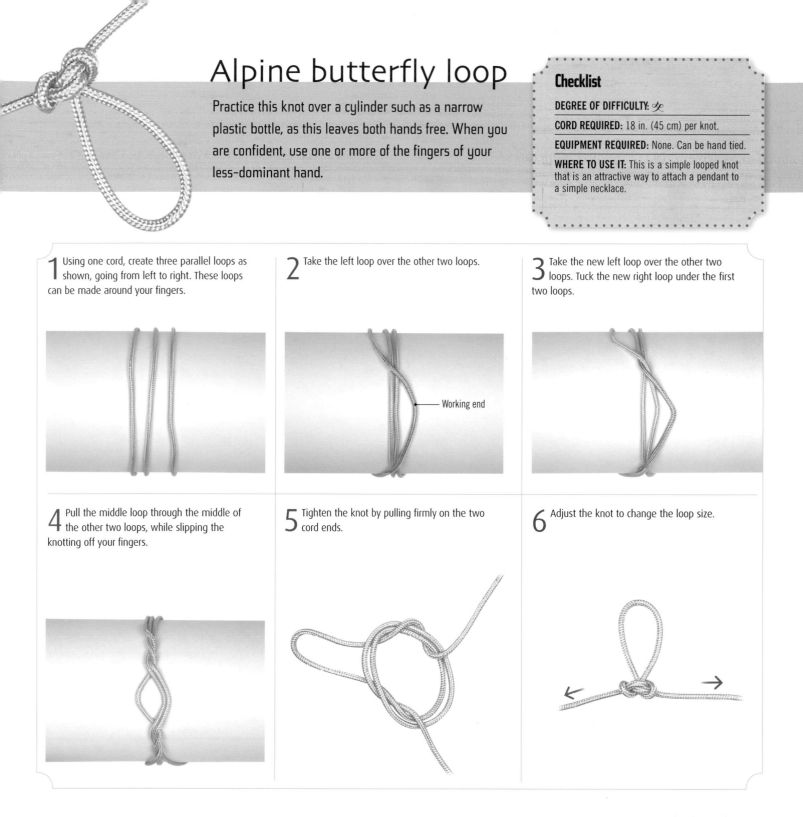

1 Using one cord, create three parallel loops as shown, going from left to right. These loops can be made around your fingers.

2 Take the left loop over the other two loops.

Working end

3 Take the new left loop over the other two loops. Tuck the new right loop under the first two loops.

4 Pull the middle loop through the middle of the other two loops, while slipping the knotting off your fingers.

5 Tighten the knot by pulling firmly on the two cord ends.

6 Adjust the knot to change the loop size.

Jury mast knot

A jury mast knot is a good starting knot for a piece of jewelry because the middle loop can be pulled out to use over a large bead or button at the other end as a fastener, or it can be pulled in to give a flat finish.

Checklist

DEGREE OF DIFFICULTY: ✎

CORD REQUIRED: 12 in. (30 cm) per knot.

EQUIPMENT REQUIRED: None. Can be hand tied.

WHERE TO USE IT: This pretty three-looped knot can be used as a focal knot, with or without beads.

1 Create three loops with the cord, tucking each new loop under the one previously made.

2 Take hold of the insides of the first and third loops and draw the two loops to either side.

3 Pull the top loop up to create a larger loop at the top of the knot.

4 To tighten the knot, pull evenly on the three loops, keeping them even in size.

VARIATIONS

1 Leather with beads on the loops and tails.

2 Top loop pulled in.

Double overhand knot

You tie a single overhand knot whenever you tie your shoes. This version is both more decorative and more secure, and is also called a surgeon's knot, since it is sometimes used to tie off sutures.

Checklist

DEGREE OF DIFFICULTY: ✀

CORD REQUIRED: 4 in. (10 cm) per knot.

EQUIPMENT REQUIRED: None. Can be hand tied.

WHERE TO USE IT: Straightforward knot that can be used to add interest to a single strand of cord. Can be combined with beads.

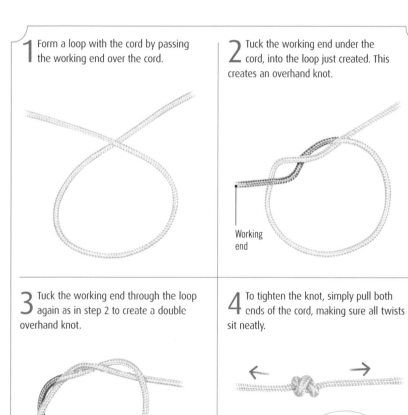

1 Form a loop with the cord by passing the working end over the cord.

2 Tuck the working end under the cord, into the loop just created. This creates an overhand knot.

Working end

3 Tuck the working end through the loop again as in step 2 to create a double overhand knot.

4 To tighten the knot, simply pull both ends of the cord, making sure all twists sit neatly.

VARIATIONS

1 Used to separate charms for a bracelet.

2 Thick, flat cord shows the knot well.

Crown knot

Crown knots are used as the basis for several knots in this section and the firecracker knot (see page 29) is a four-strand crown knot. Crown knots can be tied with anything from three strands upward.

Checklist

DEGREE OF DIFFICULTY:

CORD REQUIRED: 2 in. (5 cm) per cord per knot.

EQUIPMENT REQUIRED: Pins and a board are useful to anchor this knot to start it off.

WHERE TO USE IT: Repeating knot; can be used to create chunky bracelets.

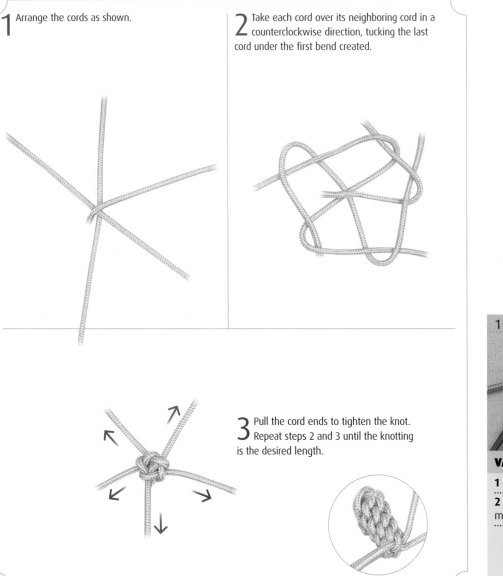

1 Arrange the cords as shown.

2 Take each cord over its neighboring cord in a counterclockwise direction, tucking the last cord under the first bend created.

3 Pull the cord ends to tighten the knot. Repeat steps 2 and 3 until the knotting is the desired length.

VARIATIONS

1 Three different-colored cords.

2 Flat cord to make a wider knot without more thickness.

Complex crown knot

A complex crown knot was traditionally used to create a tighter, more stable knot when tied around something.

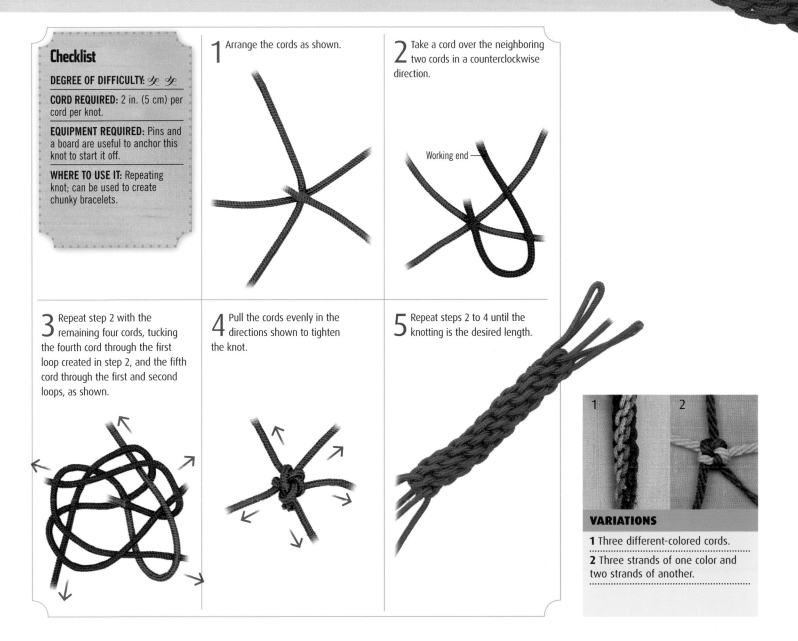

Checklist

DEGREE OF DIFFICULTY:

CORD REQUIRED: 2 in. (5 cm) per cord per knot.

EQUIPMENT REQUIRED: Pins and a board are useful to anchor this knot to start it off.

WHERE TO USE IT: Repeating knot; can be used to create chunky bracelets.

1 Arrange the cords as shown.

2 Take a cord over the neighboring two cords in a counterclockwise direction.

Working end

3 Repeat step 2 with the remaining four cords, tucking the fourth cord through the first loop created in step 2, and the fifth cord through the first and second loops, as shown.

4 Pull the cords evenly in the directions shown to tighten the knot.

5 Repeat steps 2 to 4 until the knotting is the desired length.

VARIATIONS

1 Three different-colored cords.

2 Three strands of one color and two strands of another.

Wall knot

A wall knot could be described as an upside-down crown knot (see page 64). The two knots are often combined to create button and globe knots for both practical and decorative purposes.

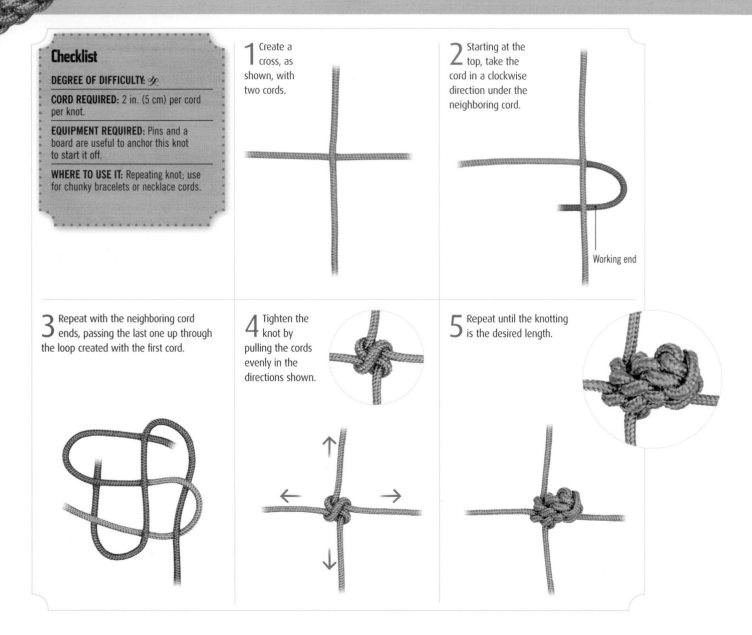

Checklist

DEGREE OF DIFFICULTY:

CORD REQUIRED: 2 in. (5 cm) per cord per knot.

EQUIPMENT REQUIRED: Pins and a board are useful to anchor this knot to start it off.

WHERE TO USE IT: Repeating knot; use for chunky bracelets or necklace cords.

1 Create a cross, as shown, with two cords.

2 Starting at the top, take the cord in a clockwise direction under the neighboring cord.

Working end

3 Repeat with the neighboring cord ends, passing the last one up through the loop created with the first cord.

4 Tighten the knot by pulling the cords evenly in the directions shown.

5 Repeat until the knotting is the desired length.

Complex wall knot

A complex wall knot is a variation of a regular wall knot (see opposite). Wall knots can be tied with a varying number of strands, from three upward. Experiment with different colors to create different effects.

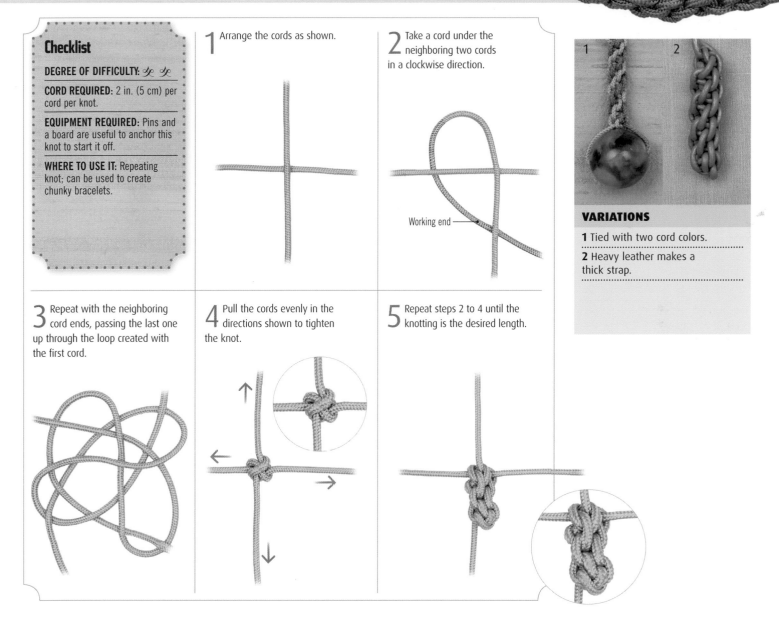

Checklist

DEGREE OF DIFFICULTY: 🏵 🏵

CORD REQUIRED: 2 in. (5 cm) per cord per knot.

EQUIPMENT REQUIRED: Pins and a board are useful to anchor this knot to start it off.

WHERE TO USE IT: Repeating knot; can be used to create chunky bracelets.

1 Arrange the cords as shown.

2 Take a cord under the neighboring two cords in a clockwise direction.

Working end

3 Repeat with the neighboring cord ends, passing the last one up through the loop created with the first cord.

4 Pull the cords evenly in the directions shown to tighten the knot.

5 Repeat steps 2 to 4 until the knotting is the desired length.

VARIATIONS

1 Tied with two cord colors.

2 Heavy leather makes a thick strap.

Epaulette knot

The épaulette knot is loosely based on a Josephine knot but extended at the sides. It works best when tied with stiffer cords—smoother cords allow the threads to move, spoiling the shape of the knot. Good as a focal knot or tied in sequence.

Checklist

DEGREE OF DIFFICULTY: ✂ ✂

CORD REQUIRED: 24 in. (60 cm) per knot.

EQUIPMENT REQUIRED: Pins and a board.

WHERE TO USE IT: A focal knot, or tied in sequence to make wide bracelets or a "bib" necklace.

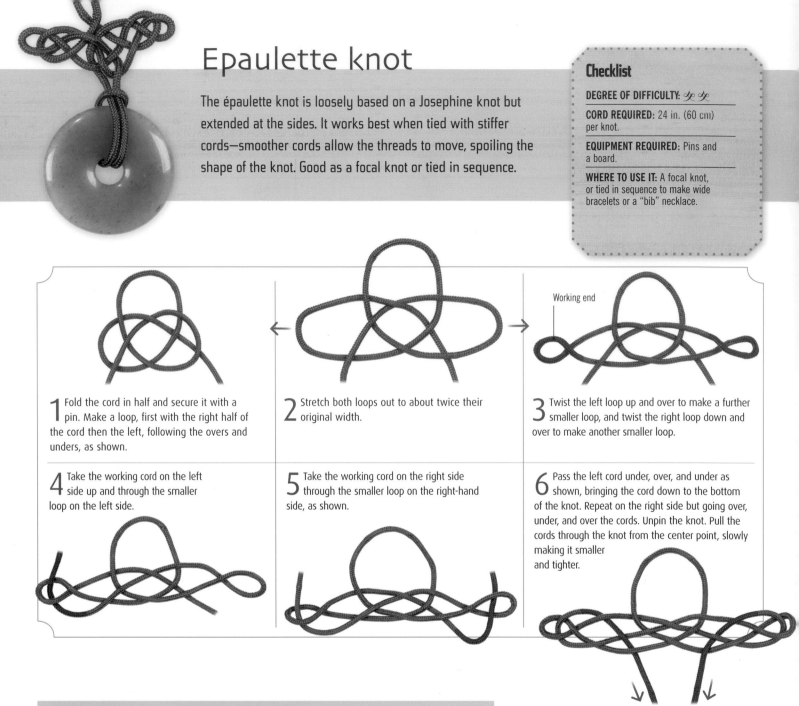

1 Fold the cord in half and secure it with a pin. Make a loop, first with the right half of the cord then the left, following the overs and unders, as shown.

2 Stretch both loops out to about twice their original width.

Working end

3 Twist the left loop up and over to make a further smaller loop, and twist the right loop down and over to make another smaller loop.

4 Take the working cord on the left side up and through the smaller loop on the left side.

5 Take the working cord on the right side through the smaller loop on the right-hand side, as shown.

6 Pass the left cord under, over, and under as shown, bringing the cord down to the bottom of the knot. Repeat on the right side but going over, under, and over the cords. Unpin the knot. Pull the cords through the knot from the center point, slowly making it smaller and tighter.

VARIATIONS

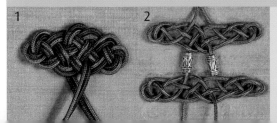

1

2

1 Double knot using two different-colored cords.

2 Tied in sequence.

Footrope knot

The footrope knot was traditionally tied to create a foothold in the ropes that sailors stood on when loosing or furling sails. For decorative purposes it makes a nice gathering knot.

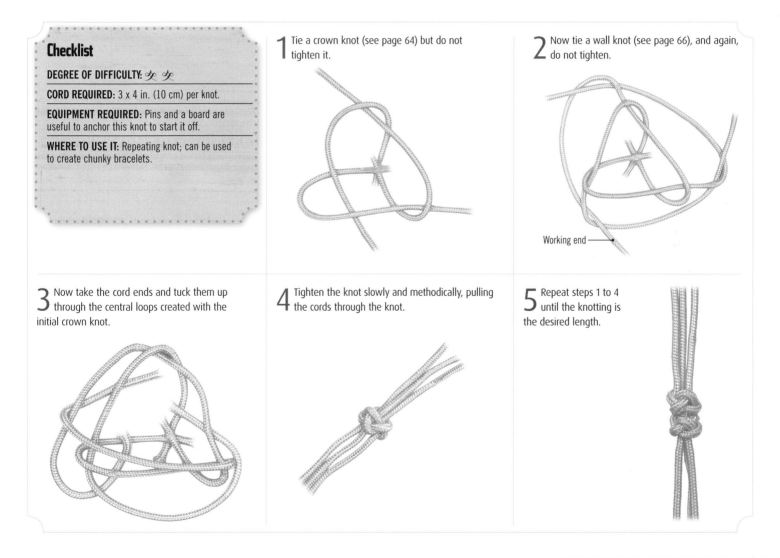

Checklist

DEGREE OF DIFFICULTY:

CORD REQUIRED: 3 x 4 in. (10 cm) per knot.

EQUIPMENT REQUIRED: Pins and a board are useful to anchor this knot to start it off.

WHERE TO USE IT: Repeating knot; can be used to create chunky bracelets.

1 Tie a crown knot (see page 64) but do not tighten it.

2 Now tie a wall knot (see page 66), and again, do not tighten.

Working end

3 Now take the cord ends and tuck them up through the central loops created with the initial crown knot.

4 Tighten the knot slowly and methodically, pulling the cords through the knot.

5 Repeat steps 1 to 4 until the knotting is the desired length.

Matthew Walker knot

This knot is simple to tie and makes a nice gathering knot between other knots or beads.

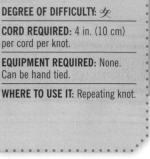

Checklist

DEGREE OF DIFFICULTY: ✂

CORD REQUIRED: 4 in. (10 cm) per cord per knot.

EQUIPMENT REQUIRED: None. Can be hand tied.

WHERE TO USE IT: Repeating knot.

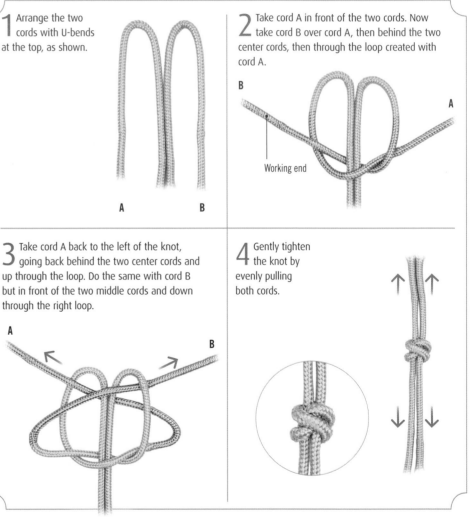

1 Arrange the two cords with U-bends at the top, as shown.

A   B

2 Take cord A in front of the two cords. Now take cord B over cord A, then behind the two center cords, then through the loop created with cord A.

B

Working end

A

3 Take cord A back to the left of the knot, going back behind the two center cords and up through the loop. Do the same with cord B but in front of the two middle cords and down through the right loop.

A

B

4 Gently tighten the knot by evenly pulling both cords.

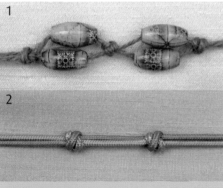

VARIATIONS

1 A rustic look using garden twine and wooden beads.

2 Two different-colored cords.

Manrope knot

This knot can be tied using between three and five strands of cord. It is a combination knot made up of a wall knot (see page 66) and a crown knot (see page 64).

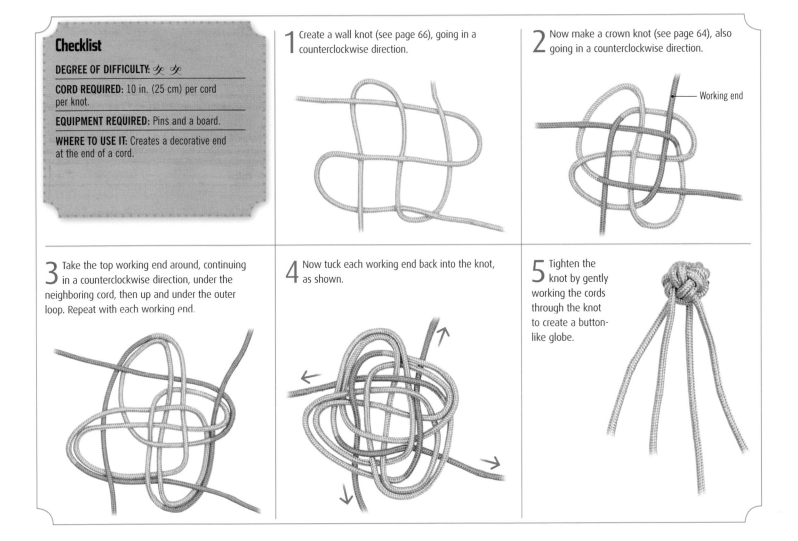

Checklist

DEGREE OF DIFFICULTY: ✂ ✂

CORD REQUIRED: 10 in. (25 cm) per cord per knot.

EQUIPMENT REQUIRED: Pins and a board.

WHERE TO USE IT: Creates a decorative end at the end of a cord.

1 Create a wall knot (see page 66), going in a counterclockwise direction.

2 Now make a crown knot (see page 64), also going in a counterclockwise direction.

— Working end

3 Take the top working end around, continuing in a counterclockwise direction, under the neighboring cord, then up and under the outer loop. Repeat with each working end.

4 Now tuck each working end back into the knot, as shown.

5 Tighten the knot by gently working the cords through the knot to create a button-like globe.

Star knot

This knot is another wall knot (see page 66) and crown knot (see page 64) combination but with a twist or two! It looks complicated to start with but once tied a couple of times is easy to master.

Checklist

DEGREE OF DIFFICULTY:

CORD REQUIRED: 12 in. (30 cm) per cord per knot.

EQUIPMENT REQUIRED: Pins and a board.

WHERE TO USE IT: Another stopper knot like the manrope knot (see page 71); makes pretty earrings.

1 Create a wall knot (see page 66) in a counterclockwise direction, but loop each cord in an underhand loop before passing it over the neighboring cord.

2 Now make a crown knot (see page 64) by passing the cord back on itself under the neighboring cord. Work in a clockwise direction, repeating with all cords.

Working end

3 Now work in a counterclockwise direction and take each cord back through the knot following its original loop, through the knot past its neighboring loop, then down through the next loop. Repeat with all cord ends.

4 Tuck each end back up through to the top of the knot, through the hole to the right of each cord.

5 The knot can be left as step 4, with cords coming out the top and bottom, or you can loop the top cords back through the outer loops so all the cords come out of the bottom of the knot. They can then be trimmed and glued in place.

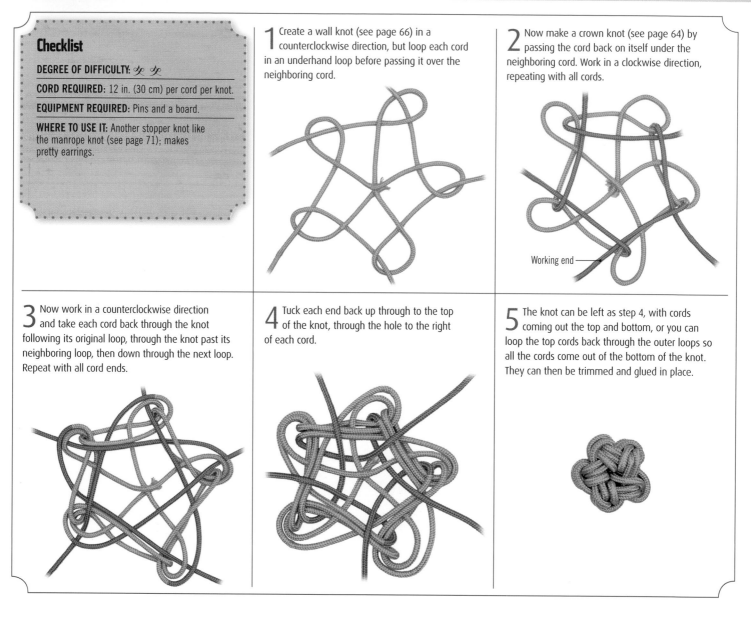

Planet Earth knot

This knot was named because it creates a not-quite-spherical shape that is flattened at the top and bottom, as is our planet.

1 Start in the center of the knot and create a loop to the right of the knot, then take the cord round to create a loop on the left of the knot, taking the working end under the cord. Now create a third loop at the bottom of the knot, still taking the cord under the knot pattern already made.

2 Take the cord around in a large loop at the top and then bring it down to the bottom of the knot under the knot pattern, then through the knot, following the overs and unders, as shown.

Working end

3 Create a fourth large outer loop and take the cord through the knot to the starting point, ensuring all overs and unders are correct.

4 Tighten the knot to shape by pulling the cord through the knot.

5 If desired the knot can be doubled or tripled by following the cord around the original knot pattern.

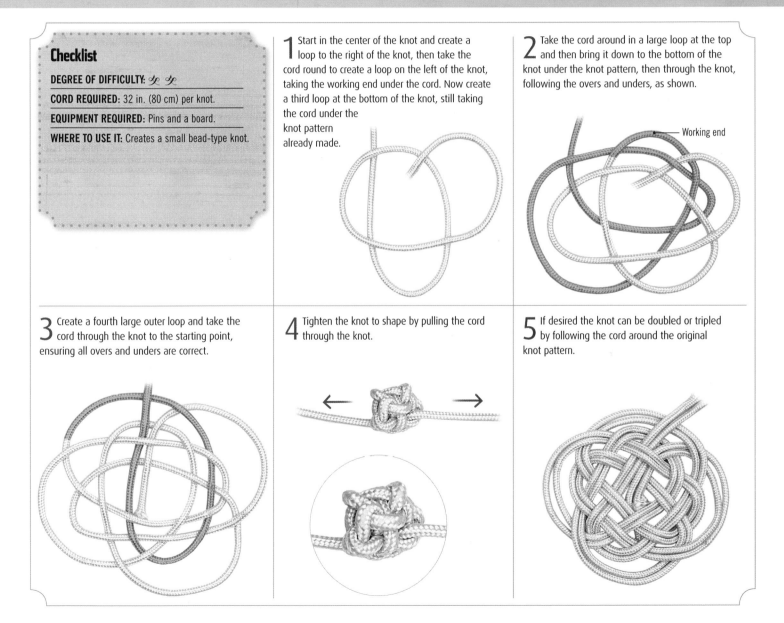

Uranus knot

This knot is a larger version of the planet Earth knot (see page 73) and is appropriately named after a larger planet. It creates a spherical ball that can be used as a bead.

Checklist

DEGREE OF DIFFICULTY: ✂ ✂

CORD REQUIRED: 2 x 60 in. (1.5m) per knot.

EQUIPMENT REQUIRED: Pins, a board, and a photocopy of the knot pattern (see page 124).

WHERE TO USE IT: Bead knot.

1 Photocopy the template on page 124. Pin the photocopy to the board. Begin at the center and follow the pattern with the cord.

2 Continue following the pattern around the knot with the cord, pinning it down as you go.

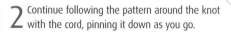
Working end

3 Ensure all the overs and unders are correct when you have completed the knotting.

4 Now take the cord around the pattern of the knot again to double it. Ensure the pattern is followed exactly and the second cord lies flat and parallel to the first with no twists.

5 Tighten the knot by pulling the cords through the knot until it takes the correct shape.

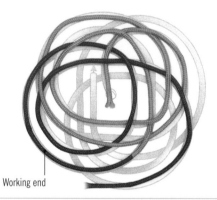

Flat Turk's head knot

At the center of this knot is a six-pointed star, composed of two triangles. The upward-pointing triangle symbolizes fire and the downward-pointing one symbolizes water. The star is known as the seal of Solomon.

Checklist

DEGREE OF DIFFICULTY: ✿ ✿

CORD REQUIRED: 43 in. (1.1 m) per knot (or 2 x 22 in./55 cm cords).

EQUIPMENT REQUIRED: Pins and a board.

WHERE TO USE IT: Pendant knot; pretty on necklaces or bracelets.

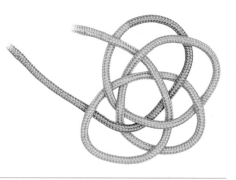

1 Create two loops with the cord, taking the second one underneath the first one and bringing the cord up and over the start of the first loop.

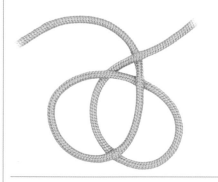

2 Make a third loop following the under, over, under, over, and under pattern, as shown.

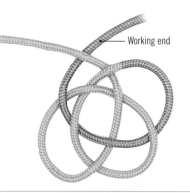

Working end

3 Now take the cord round to create another loop, this time going under, over, under, under, over, under, and over through the knot pattern.

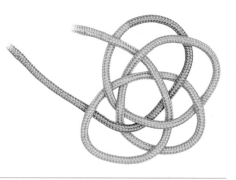

4 Complete the knot pattern by making a fifth loop, then take the cord in a repeating under-and-over pattern through the knot back to the start point.

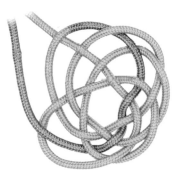

5 Take the cord round for a second time, exactly following the path of the initial knot pattern, ensuring the cords don't twist. A second colored cord can be used.

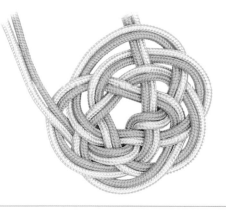

6 Tighten the knot by gently pulling the cords through the knot.

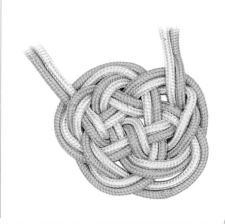

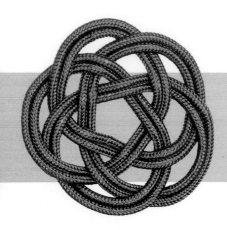

Four-lead, five-bight Turk's head knot

This pretty knot was originally designed to be tied flat, then tightened around something to make a tubular knot, but it also looks very pretty when left flat.

Checklist

DEGREE OF DIFFICULTY:

CORD REQUIRED: 39 in. (1 m) per knot.

EQUIPMENT REQUIRED: Pins and a board.

WHERE TO USE IT: A pretty, Celtic-style focal knot. Can be used to make brooches.

1 Create a loop with the cord, as shown.

2 Make a second loop at the top of the knot, then bring the cord down through the knot, going under, over, and then under the previously made loop.

— Working end

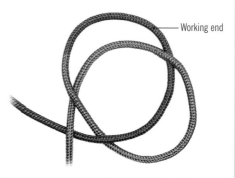

3 Create a third loop on the left of the knot, lacing the cord through the two previously created loops, ensuring the overs and unders are correct.

4 Complete the knot pattern by taking the cord through the knot, alternating the over and under pattern until the cord is back at the knot starting point.

5 Take the cord around again to double the knot, then tighten it by pulling the cord slowly and gently through the knot until all the loops are even.

Turk's head braid

This knot creates a multistranded braided pattern but only uses one cord. Tie around different-size centers to create different-size tubes. Smaller centers and a smaller diameter cord can be used to create a ring.

1 Make a loop around the tube, crossing the cord over at the front.

2 Make a second loop around the tube, coming back to the front in between the two loops, then crossing it over the second one at point A. Pin this cross in place. Pass the cord under the first loop created and over the second one.

3 Rotate the knotting toward you and pull the first loop created over the second one, creating two new crossing points at B and C.

4 Take the cord end and pass it through the loop just created, going under then over the cord. Then loop the cord back to the left, coming up between the two cords at the bottom.

5 Now repeat steps 3 and 4 until the cord is back at the starting point.

6 Complete the braid by following the original pattern around a second and third time to create a three-strand braid pattern.

Blimp knot

This knot is easy to tie and can be repeated in a single length of cord, interspersed with beads to make a simple bracelet.

Checklist

DEGREE OF DIFFICULTY:

CORD REQUIRED: 12 in. (30 cm) per knot.

EQUIPMENT REQUIRED: None. Can be hand tied.

WHERE TO USE IT: Simple, symmetrical knot to intersperse with beads.

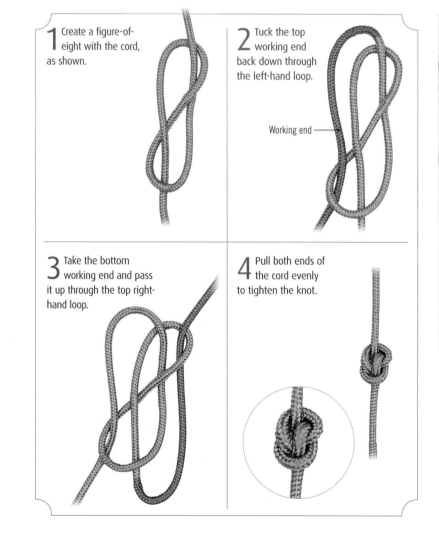

1 Create a figure-of-eight with the cord, as shown.

2 Tuck the top working end back down through the left-hand loop.

Working end

3 Take the bottom working end and pass it up through the top right-hand loop.

4 Pull both ends of the cord evenly to tighten the knot.

1

2

VARIATIONS

1 Leather knots with small glass beads for highlights.

2 Flat braid, knots tied one to the left and the other to the right.

Braid knot

This knot creates a pretty braided effect using only one length of cord. It is more stable when doubled.

Checklist

DEGREE OF DIFFICULTY: ✄

CORD REQUIRED: 12 in. (30 cm) of cord will make approximately 2¼ in. (6 cm) of braid.

EQUIPMENT REQUIRED: None. Can be hand tied.

WHERE TO USE IT: Use to create short sections of braiding between beads or other knots.

1 Create a U-bend around the cord to create a large loop, as shown.

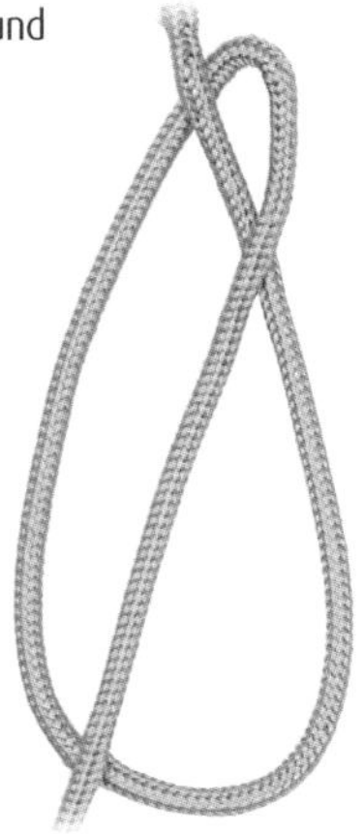

2 Take the left-hand cord over the loose end of cord to the middle. Now take the right-hand cord over the left one to start the braid.

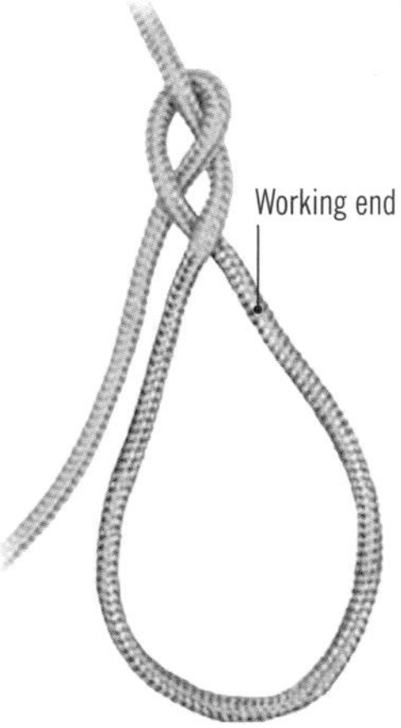

Working end

3 Take the right side of the loop over the left to make two spaces, as shown. Put the loose end through the first space from the left and the second from the right.

4 Repeat step 3 to continue the braid. Continue until you reach the bottom of the loop, pull the cord through the loop, and tighten.

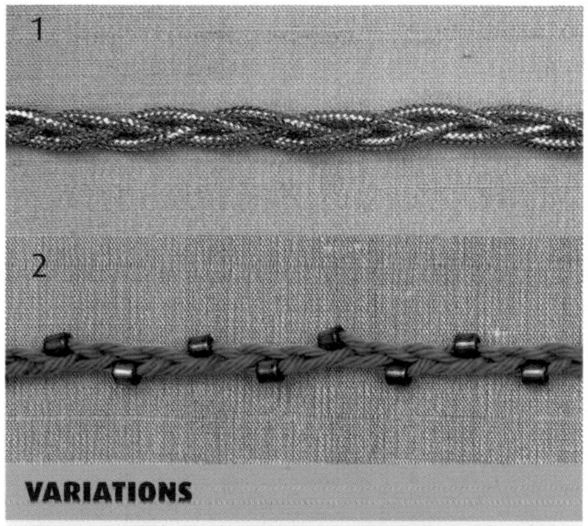

VARIATIONS

1 Gold cord braid looks like metal chain.

2 Beads on the working cord.

Double chain

This double chain is sometimes called a doubled trumpet or bugle cord due to its use on bandsmen's uniforms.

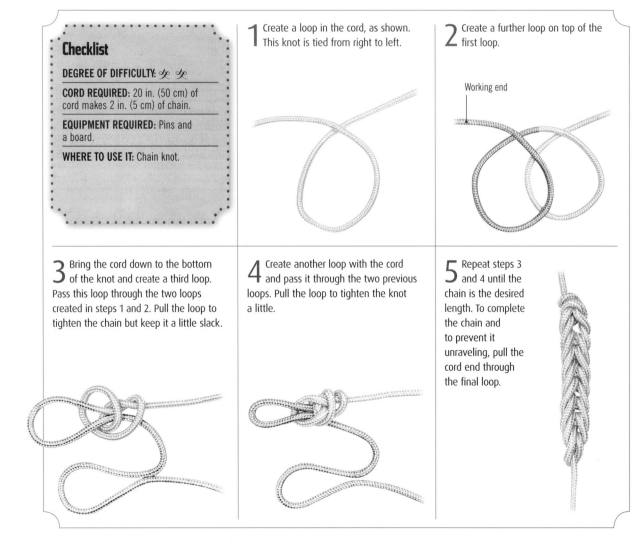

Checklist

DEGREE OF DIFFICULTY:

CORD REQUIRED: 20 in. (50 cm) of cord makes 2 in. (5 cm) of chain.

EQUIPMENT REQUIRED: Pins and a board.

WHERE TO USE IT: Chain knot.

1 Create a loop in the cord, as shown. This knot is tied from right to left.

2 Create a further loop on top of the first loop.

Working end

3 Bring the cord down to the bottom of the knot and create a third loop. Pass this loop through the two loops created in steps 1 and 2. Pull the loop to tighten the chain but keep it a little slack.

4 Create another loop with the cord and pass it through the two previous loops. Pull the loop to tighten the knot a little.

5 Repeat steps 3 and 4 until the chain is the desired length. To complete the chain and to prevent it unraveling, pull the cord end through the final loop.

Zigzag braid

This is a simple braid that creates an interesting textured effect. Not seen as often as a three-stranded plait, it's something different for bracelets or necklace cords.

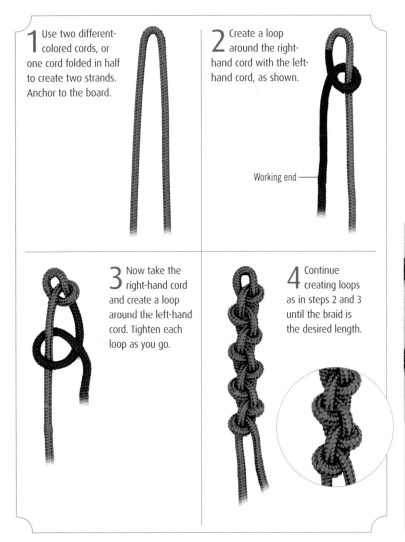

1 Use two different-colored cords, or one cord folded in half to create two strands. Anchor to the board.

2 Create a loop around the right-hand cord with the left-hand cord, as shown.

Working end

3 Now take the right-hand cord and create a loop around the left-hand cord. Tighten each loop as you go.

4 Continue creating loops as in steps 2 and 3 until the braid is the desired length.

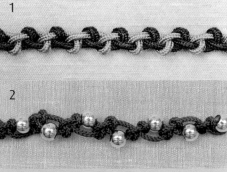

VARIATIONS

1 Two colors of cord.

2 Bead added between pairs of knots.

Three-strand plait

Most people will recognize the pattern created with a three-stranded plait. Use three different colors to create interest. Use contrasting colors to make a statement or complementary colors for a more subtle effect.

Checklist

DEGREE OF DIFFICULTY: ✂

CORD REQUIRED: 3 x 4-in. (10-cm) cords make approx. 2¼ in. (6 cm) of plait.

EQUIPMENT REQUIRED: Hand tied but it is useful to anchor the plait.

WHERE TO USE IT: Simple plait for bracelets.

1 Anchor the three cords together at the top and lay them flat and parallel to each other, as shown.

A   B   C

2 Take cord A and pass it over cord B.

3 Now take cord C and take it over cord A to lie between cords A and B.

4 Complete one sequence of the plait by taking cord B and passing it over cord C to lie between cords A and C.

5 Repeat steps 2 to 4 until the plait is the desired length.

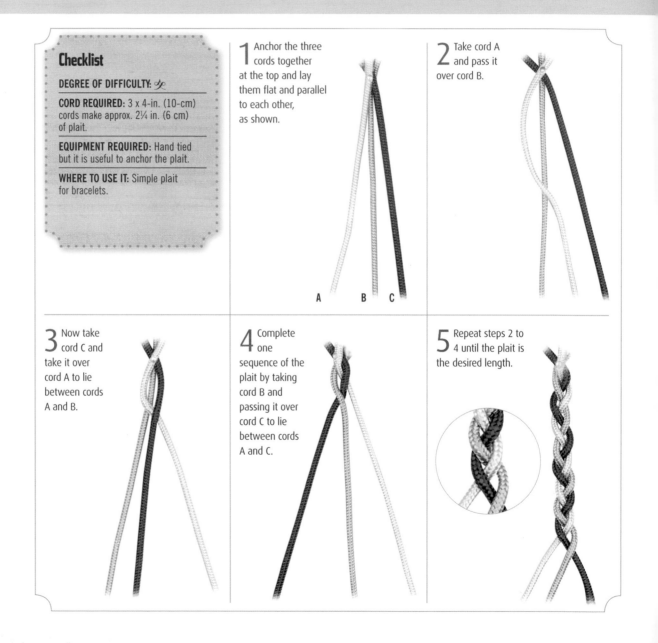

Four-strand plait

This plait creates a pretty, solid cord that would make an attractive necklace cord to hang a pendant on. One or two colors can be used.

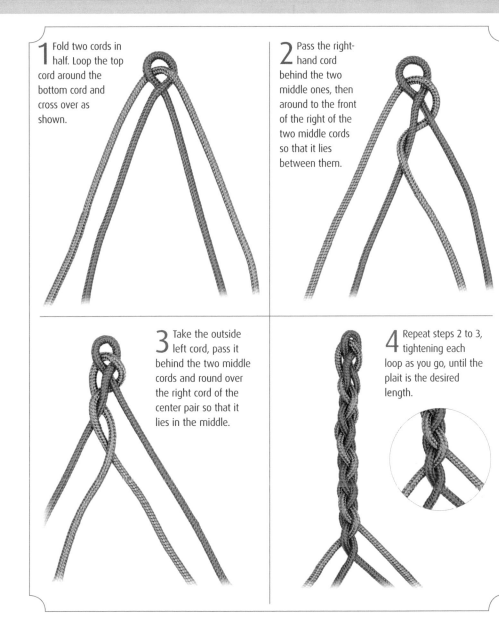

1 Fold two cords in half. Loop the top cord around the bottom cord and cross over as shown.

2 Pass the right-hand cord behind the two middle ones, then around to the front of the right of the two middle cords so that it lies between them.

3 Take the outside left cord, pass it behind the two middle cords and round over the right cord of the center pair so that it lies in the middle.

4 Repeat steps 2 to 3, tightening each loop as you go, until the plait is the desired length.

VARIATIONS

1 Double strands of four colors of embroidery thread.

2 Two colors of flat braid create a striped pattern.

Four-strand braid

This is an extended version of a three-strand plait (see page 82), creating a flat braid. It can be created with four different-colored cords that would need to be gathered at the top before starting the braiding.

Checklist

DEGREE OF DIFFICULTY: ✍

CORD REQUIRED: 2 x 8-in. (20-cm) cords make approx. 2¼ in. (6 cm) of braid.

EQUIPMENT REQUIRED: This braid requires an anchor while it is being tied.

WHERE TO USE IT: Attractive flat braid, well suited to using with beads.

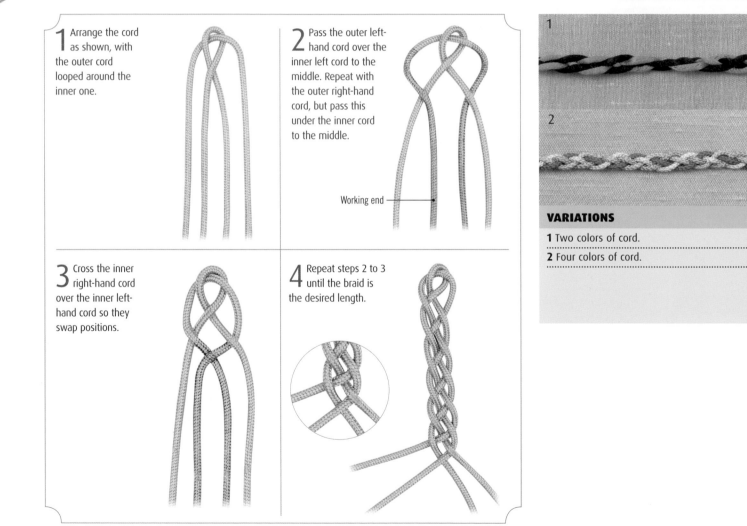

1 Arrange the cord as shown, with the outer cord looped around the inner one.

2 Pass the outer left-hand cord over the inner left cord to the middle. Repeat with the outer right-hand cord, but pass this under the inner cord to the middle.

Working end

3 Cross the inner right-hand cord over the inner left-hand cord so they swap positions.

4 Repeat steps 2 to 3 until the braid is the desired length.

VARIATIONS

1 Two colors of cord.

2 Four colors of cord.

Six-strand plait

This plait is created with a similar method to creating crown knots in that the cords are passed over one another. It is not exactly the same though, and takes some concentrating to ensure the correct cords are being used at the correct time.

Checklist

DEGREE OF DIFFICULTY: ✀ ✀

CORD REQUIRED: 3 x 8-in. (20-cm) cords make approx. 1½ in. (4 cm) of plait.

EQUIPMENT REQUIRED: Pins and a board.

WHERE TO USE IT: Chunky plait for use as bracelets or necklace cords.

1 Arrange the three cords as shown. This plait can be made with six different-colored cords if you want to create an interesting effect.

2 Pass every other cord over its neighbor in a counterclockwise direction.

Working end

3 Now take the three cords that were the lazy cords in step 2 and pass them over the neighboring cord in a clockwise direction.

4 Repeat steps 2 to 3 until the plait is the desired length. Ensure you keep the two groups of three working ends separate.

VARIATIONS

1 Three strands in each of two colors.

2 Two strands in each of three colors.

Phoenix tail knot

The phoenix tail knot is made up of a series of chain knots made using two cords. It can be tied using two different-colored cords, showing the structure of the knot very well.

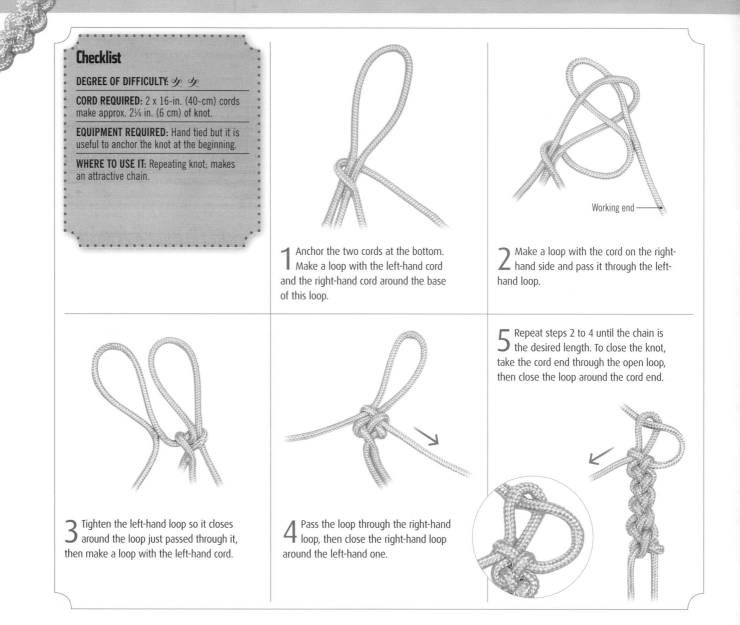

Checklist

DEGREE OF DIFFICULTY:

CORD REQUIRED: 2 x 16-in. (40-cm) cords make approx. 2¼ in. (6 cm) of knot.

EQUIPMENT REQUIRED: Hand tied but it is useful to anchor the knot at the beginning.

WHERE TO USE IT: Repeating knot; makes an attractive chain.

1 Anchor the two cords at the bottom. Make a loop with the left-hand cord and the right-hand cord around the base of this loop.

2 Make a loop with the cord on the right-hand side and pass it through the left-hand loop.

Working end

3 Tighten the left-hand loop so it closes around the loop just passed through it, then make a loop with the left-hand cord.

4 Pass the loop through the right-hand loop, then close the right-hand loop around the left-hand one.

5 Repeat steps 2 to 4 until the chain is the desired length. To close the knot, take the cord end through the open loop, then close the loop around the cord end.

Ring hitching

There are several types of ring hitching. The one demonstrated here is called ringbolt hitching. Ring hitching was traditionally used to cover metal rings bolted to the deck of a ship.

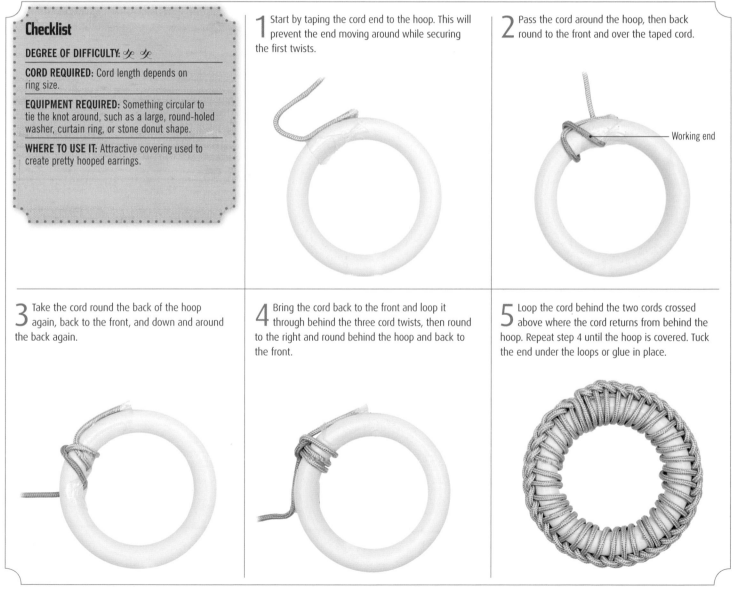

Checklist

DEGREE OF DIFFICULTY: ✎ ✎

CORD REQUIRED: Cord length depends on ring size.

EQUIPMENT REQUIRED: Something circular to tie the knot around, such as a large, round-holed washer, curtain ring, or stone donut shape.

WHERE TO USE IT: Attractive covering used to create pretty hooped earrings.

1 Start by taping the cord end to the hoop. This will prevent the end moving around while securing the first twists.

2 Pass the cord around the hoop, then back round to the front and over the taped cord.

Working end

3 Take the cord round the back of the hoop again, back to the front, and down and around the back again.

4 Bring the cord back to the front and loop it through behind the three cord twists, then round to the right and round behind the hoop and back to the front.

5 Loop the cord behind the two cords crossed above where the cord returns from behind the hoop. Repeat step 4 until the hoop is covered. Tuck the end under the loops or glue in place.

Spanish hitching

Using one or more colored strands of cord clearly shows the movement of each cord around the chunky cylinder created.

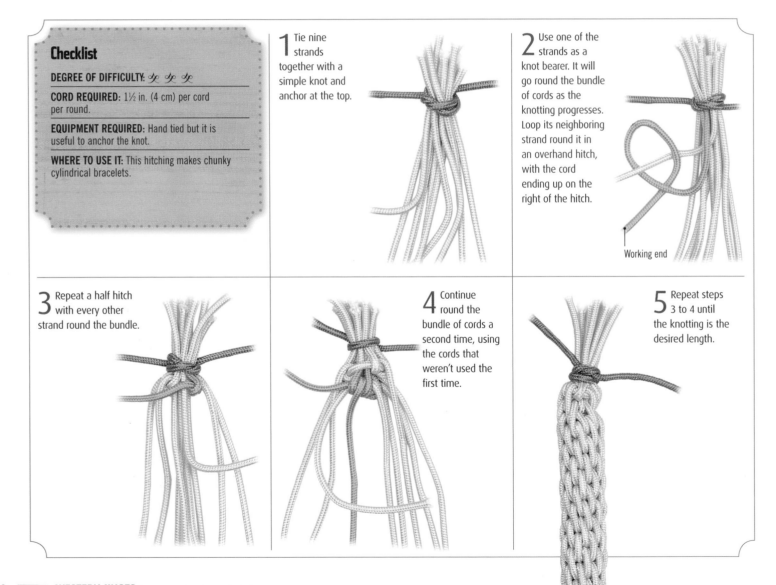

Checklist

DEGREE OF DIFFICULTY: ✎ ✎ ✎

CORD REQUIRED: 1½ in. (4 cm) per cord per round.

EQUIPMENT REQUIRED: Hand tied but it is useful to anchor the knot.

WHERE TO USE IT: This hitching makes chunky cylindrical bracelets.

1 Tie nine strands together with a simple knot and anchor at the top.

2 Use one of the strands as a knot bearer. It will go round the bundle of cords as the knotting progresses. Loop its neighboring strand round it in an overhand hitch, with the cord ending up on the right of the hitch.

Working end

3 Repeat a half hitch with every other strand round the bundle.

4 Continue round the bundle of cords a second time, using the cords that weren't used the first time.

5 Repeat steps 3 to 4 until the knotting is the desired length.

Eight-plait grommet

This knot is one of those that sometimes takes forever to make and sometimes can be done in as little as 20 minutes. When first tying this knot it is easier to use two different-colored threads.

Checklist

DEGREE OF DIFFICULTY: ✿ ✿ ✿

CORD REQUIRED: 2 x 32 in. (80 cm) per knot.

EQUIPMENT REQUIRED: None. Can be hand tied.

WHERE TO USE IT: Bead knot.

1 Tie an overhand knot, leaving a large loop, as shown.

2 Repeatedly tuck the working end round the loop until you get back to the start point.

3 Follow the path of tucks around the loop a third and fourth time, trying to keep the tucks quite loose. You should now have a four-strand grommet.

4 Take the second cord and work in the opposite direction around the loop, going under two strands and over two strands repeatedly as you go round.

5 Go round the loop a second time with the second cord, repeating the pattern of overs and unders but one strand over from the first round.

6 Going round the third and fourth time will fill in the gaps and result in an eight-strand grommet with four strands of cord protruding close to each other.

Trefoil knot

Before tying this knot it is worth mastering the eight-plait grommet (see page 89), since the method is the same. This knot is really amazing to look at and is sure to cause comment when worn.

(see page 89)

Checklist

DEGREE OF DIFFICULTY: ✎ ✎ ✎

CORD REQUIRED: 10 ft 5 in. (3.2 m) per knot.

EQUIPMENT REQUIRED: Pins and a board.

WHERE TO USE IT: Bead knot.

1 Start by making the knot shape as shown, tucking the working end under the beginning of the start point. Leave 24 in. (60 cm) of cord free on the non-working end—you will need this to finish.

2 Continue around the path of the knot, tucking the working end round until you return to the start point.

3 Continue with wrapping and tucking around the knot a third and fourth time until a four-strand grommet is made.

4 Wrap the two working ends around each other and tuck both under two strands to anchor them. Take one strand around the knot in the opposite direction to the previous working strand, going over two strands, under two strands until back at the start point.

5 Repeat step 4 with one end of the cord, then repeat twice in the other direction with the other end. The cord ends should end up close to one another and you will have an interlocked eight-strand trefoil.

Single-strand star knot

This knot is created using a modified version of linking a simple chain together to create a star shape due to the change in direction of the chain.

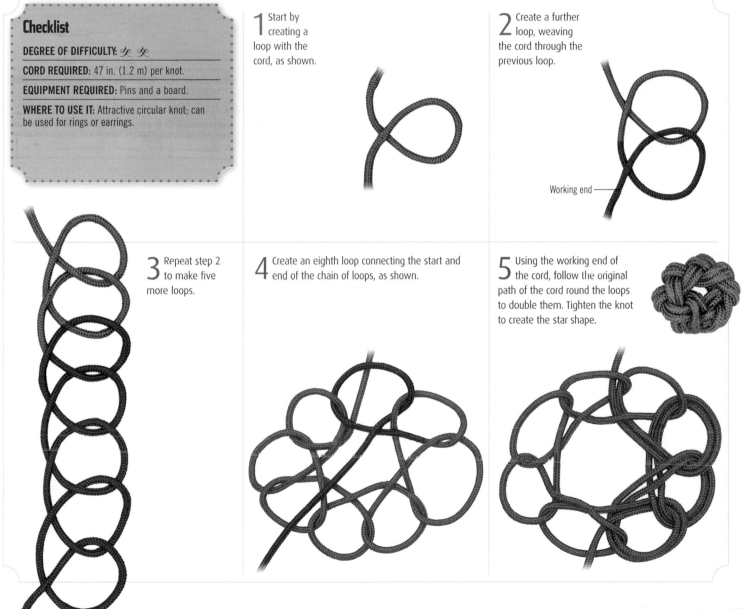

Checklist

DEGREE OF DIFFICULTY:

CORD REQUIRED: 47 in. (1.2 m) per knot.

EQUIPMENT REQUIRED: Pins and a board.

WHERE TO USE IT: Attractive circular knot; can be used for rings or earrings.

1 Start by creating a loop with the cord, as shown.

2 Create a further loop, weaving the cord through the previous loop.

Working end

3 Repeat step 2 to make five more loops.

4 Create an eighth loop connecting the start and end of the chain of loops, as shown.

5 Using the working end of the cord, follow the original path of the cord round the loops to double them. Tighten the knot to create the star shape.

Figure-of-eight chain

The continuous single line that makes up the figure-of-eight chain is a symbol of eternity and the boundlessness of God. The figure-of-eight pattern is one of the 12 elementary Celtic knots.

Checklist

DEGREE OF DIFFICULTY:

CORD REQUIRED: 6 in. (15 cm) per knot.

EQUIPMENT REQUIRED: Pins and a board make tying this knot easier.

WHERE TO USE IT: Repeating knot; can be used to make wide cuff-style bracelets.

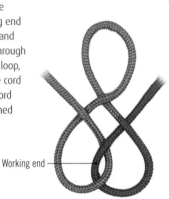

1 Create a figure-of-eight, as shown.

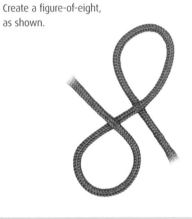

2 Take the working end of the cord and loop it up through the bottom loop, crossing the cord under the cord already pinned down.

Working end —

3 Repeat at the top to create the second loop of a second figure-of-eight.

4 Repeat steps 2 and 3 until the chain is the desired length. Doubling the chain with a second cord makes the chain more stable and looks attractive with a different color.

VARIATIONS

1 Flat braid makes a firm mat.

2 Bead at each edge loop.

Horizontal figure-of-eight chain

In this chain, the figure-of-eight is made on its side and creates a narrower chain than the figure-of-eight chain previously described. Doubling or trebling the chain with different-colored cords creates an attractive effect.

Checklist

DEGREE OF DIFFICULTY: ✁

CORD REQUIRED: 8 in. (20 cm) per knot.

EQUIPMENT REQUIRED: Pins and a board make tying this knot easier.

WHERE TO USE IT: Repeating knot; can be used to create wide necklaces.

1 Create two loops with the cord, as shown, to create a figure-of-eight on its side.

2 Take the cord to the right, going under the figure-of-eight, and create a loop with the cord going under at the neck of the loop.

Working end

3 Loop the cord over, under, then over through the right-hand loop of the first figure-of-eight to complete the second figure-of-eight.

4 Continue creating figure-of-eights until the chain is the desired length. Doubling and trebling makes the knot more stable.

VARIATIONS

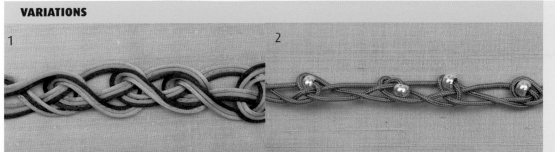

1

2

1 Three strands together.

2 Beads at the top of each loop make a stable row.

Carrick mat

Steps 1 to 3 of this knot create a knot called a full carrick bend. This knot can be left flat, as per the instructions, or the ends can be moved slightly to protrude from the knot and gathered together before creating a necklace cord with a ready-made pendant.

Checklist

DEGREE OF DIFFICULTY: ✂

CORD REQUIRED: 16 in. (40 cm) per knot.

EQUIPMENT REQUIRED: Pins and a board.

WHERE TO USE IT: Focal knot; looks attractive with a pendant.

1 Create two loops with the cord, ensuring the overs and unders are as shown.

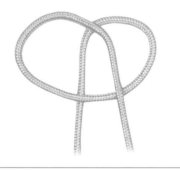

2 Create a further loop bottom left, ensuring the cord goes under, over, under, over, and under, as shown.

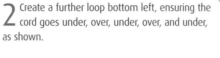
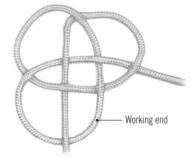

— Working end

3 Continue looping the cord round to create a fourth loop and follow the original knotting up to begin doubling the knot.

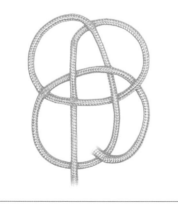

4 Continue following the knotting round a second and third time to finish the knot, making sure each subsequent repeat lies parallel to the first with no crossovers of the cord.

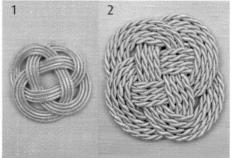

1   2

VARIATIONS

1 Stiff silver cord allows the knot to be stable when left more open.

2 Using a twisted silk cord.

Oval mat

This lovely knot develops its oval shape when it is tightened. Instead of using the same cord to double the knot, a second one of a different color could be used.

Checklist

DEGREE OF DIFFICULTY: ✎ ✎

CORD REQUIRED: 60 in. (1.5 m) per knot.

EQUIPMENT REQUIRED: Pins and a board.

WHERE TO USE IT: This knot is a focal knot and makes an attractive brooch.

1 Starting at the right of the knot, create three interlocking loops, as shown, ensuring the overs and unders are correct.

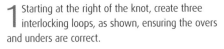

2 Create a loop with the cord and then thread it through the knot, going over, under, over, over, under, and over the knot pattern.

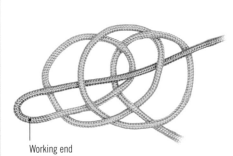

Working end

3 Create a loop on the right of the knot, then thread the cord back through the knot, going over the threaded cord from step 2 in the center of the knot.

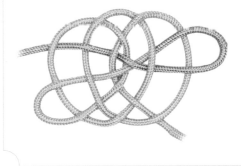

4 Make another loop on the left of the knot, then back through the knot, carefully following the overs and unders, as shown.

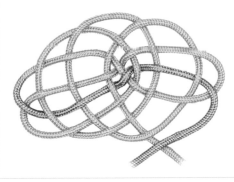

5 Double the knot by taking a second cord and follow the original cord round the knot pattern, keeping the two cords parallel. Tighten the knot by pulling the cords gently through the knot.

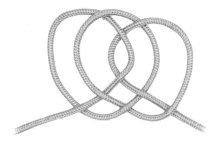

Prolong knot

This knot is also called a long mat. It lends itself naturally to being used with a pendant due to the loop created at the top. A pendant would need to be threaded onto the middle of the cord before starting the knot.

Checklist

DEGREE OF DIFFICULTY:

CORD REQUIRED: 25 in. (65 cm) per knot.

EQUIPMENT REQUIRED: Pins and a board.

WHERE TO USE IT: Focal knot; well suited to using with a pendant.

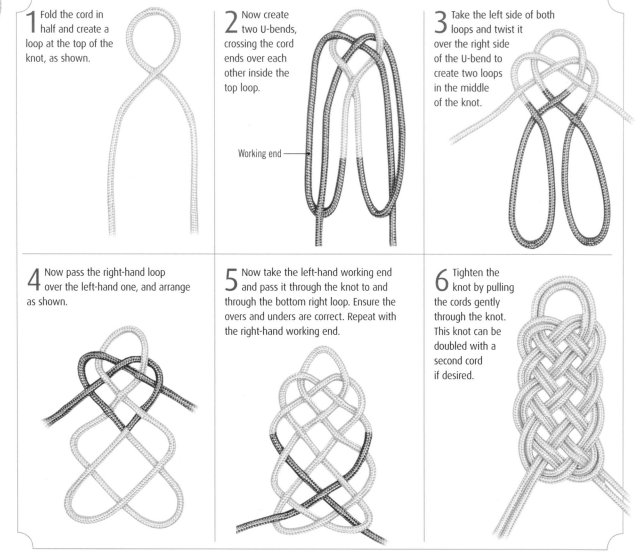

1 Fold the cord in half and create a loop at the top of the knot, as shown.

2 Now create two U-bends, crossing the cord ends over each other inside the top loop.

Working end

3 Take the left side of both loops and twist it over the right side of the U-bend to create two loops in the middle of the knot.

4 Now pass the right-hand loop over the left-hand one, and arrange as shown.

5 Now take the left-hand working end and pass it through the knot to and through the bottom right loop. Ensure the overs and unders are correct. Repeat with the right-hand working end.

6 Tighten the knot by pulling the cords gently through the knot. This knot can be doubled with a second cord if desired.

Round mat

The round mat is similar to the carrick mat (see page 94) but with five
loops, making it more stable and more decorative, with an open space
in the center that can be used to frame a bead or stone.

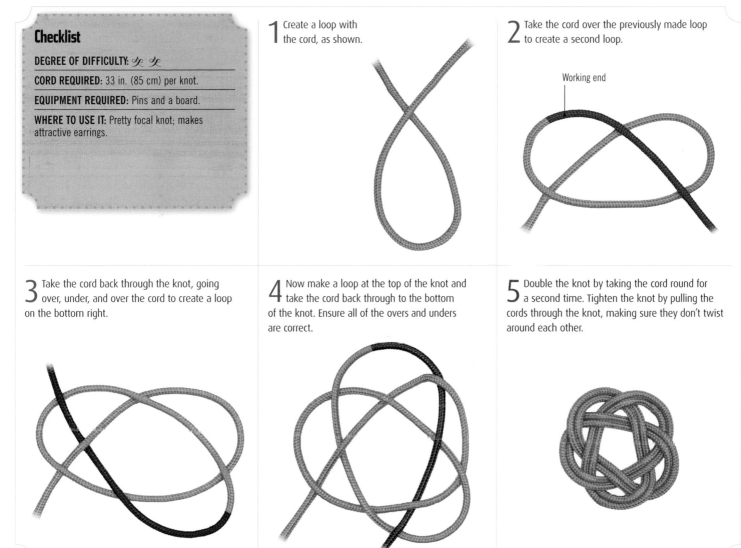

Checklist

DEGREE OF DIFFICULTY:

CORD REQUIRED: 33 in. (85 cm) per knot.

EQUIPMENT REQUIRED: Pins and a board.

WHERE TO USE IT: Pretty focal knot; makes
attractive earrings.

1 Create a loop with
the cord, as shown.

2 Take the cord over the previously made loop
to create a second loop.

Working end

3 Take the cord back through the knot, going
over, under, and over the cord to create a loop
on the bottom right.

4 Now make a loop at the top of the knot and
take the cord back through to the bottom
of the knot. Ensure all of the overs and unders
are correct.

5 Double the knot by taking the cord round for
a second time. Tighten the knot by pulling the
cords through the knot, making sure they don't twist
around each other.

Eight-strand square knot

This knot is another variation of the wall and crown knots but made using a large number of strands. The wall and crown knots in alternate directions are what create the square appearance. Creating the knots in the same direction will make a round knot.

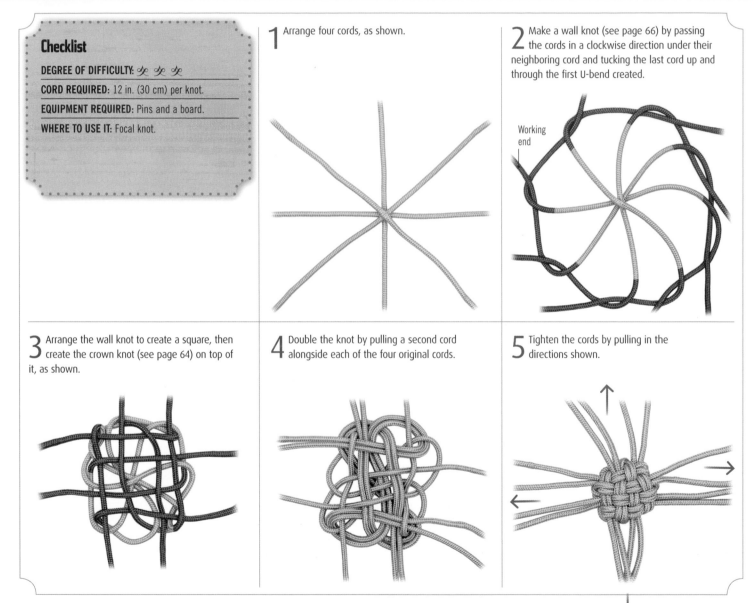

Checklist

DEGREE OF DIFFICULTY:

CORD REQUIRED: 12 in. (30 cm) per knot.

EQUIPMENT REQUIRED: Pins and a board.

WHERE TO USE IT: Focal knot.

1 Arrange four cords, as shown.

2 Make a wall knot (see page 66) by passing the cords in a clockwise direction under their neighboring cord and tucking the last cord up and through the first U-bend created.

Working end

3 Arrange the wall knot to create a square, then create the crown knot (see page 64) on top of it, as shown.

4 Double the knot by pulling a second cord alongside each of the four original cords.

5 Tighten the cords by pulling in the directions shown.

Celtic cross

The cross is an instantly recognizable symbol and Celtic symbols are often seen adorning crosses. This knot can be doubled, creating a more solid shape.

Checklist

DEGREE OF DIFFICULTY: ✂ ✂

CORD REQUIRED: 39 in. (1 m) per knot.

EQUIPMENT REQUIRED: Pins and a board.

WHERE TO USE IT: Focal knot; creates a pretty pendant.

1 You will need two cords to tie this knot. Fold the first cord in half, making a loop at the top, then make a loop either side, crossing the cords over as shown.

2 Create two further loops, alternating the cord crossovers, as shown.

— Working end

3 Now take the second cord. Start at the bottom of the knot, pass the cord between the cords crossover then create two loops back up the cross. Ensure all overs and unders are correct.

4 Make a loop on either side of the arm of the cross, taking the cord through the existing loops, checking all overs and unders are correct.

5 To complete the knot, cross the two cords over inside the top loop after threading the cords through the original knotting. Check all overs and unders are correct before tightening.

Circle of life

The circle is a symbol of eternity because of its endless shape. This knot consists of a series of intertwined loops to create the overall circular shape.

1 Create two loops, as shown.

2 Make a further loop at the top of the knot, then take the cord over the second loop created in step 1 and make another loop at the bottom of the knot.

Working end

3 Thread the cord through the knot, following the overs and unders shown to link the loops together.

4 Make another loop, going over the top of the first loop created. Take the cord back through the knot going under, over, and under previous knotting.

5 Pass the cord through the knot, creating a further loop to close the circle. Ensure the overs and unders are correct before unpinning and tightening the knot.

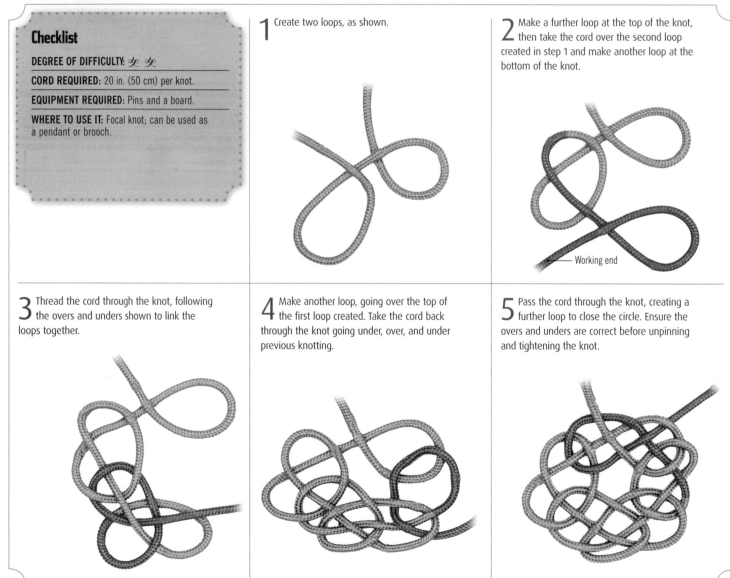

Triangular knot

Triangles are very symbolic, representing such things as the Christian Trinity, the domains of earth, sea, and sky, or mind, body, and soul. This knot is also known as the triquetra.

Checklist

DEGREE OF DIFFICULTY: 𝆓 𝆓

CORD REQUIRED: 20 in. (50 cm) per knot.

EQUIPMENT REQUIRED: Pins and a board.

WHERE TO USE IT: Focal knot; can be used as a pendant or earrings.

1 Create a large loop, as shown, making a small loop in the bottom left-hand corner.

2 Take the cord down and create a loop around the cord on the bottom right-hand corner, ensuring all the overs and unders are correct.

— Working end

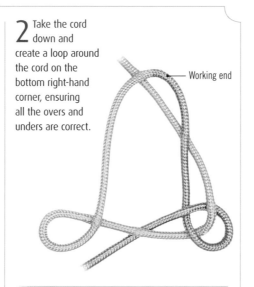

3 Complete the triangle by passing the cord through the knot, as shown.

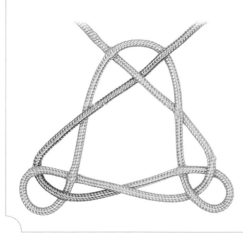

4 With a second cord, either the same color or a different one, follow the path of the original cord around the knot to double it. Ensure the two cords lie parallel to each other and don't twist.

VARIATIONS

1 Single flat cord.

2 Two colors.

Heart knot

The heart is an instantly recognizable shape and universally represents love. It is not a traditional Celtic symbol but the Celtic knotwork principle of interlacing overs and unders can be applied to many shapes.

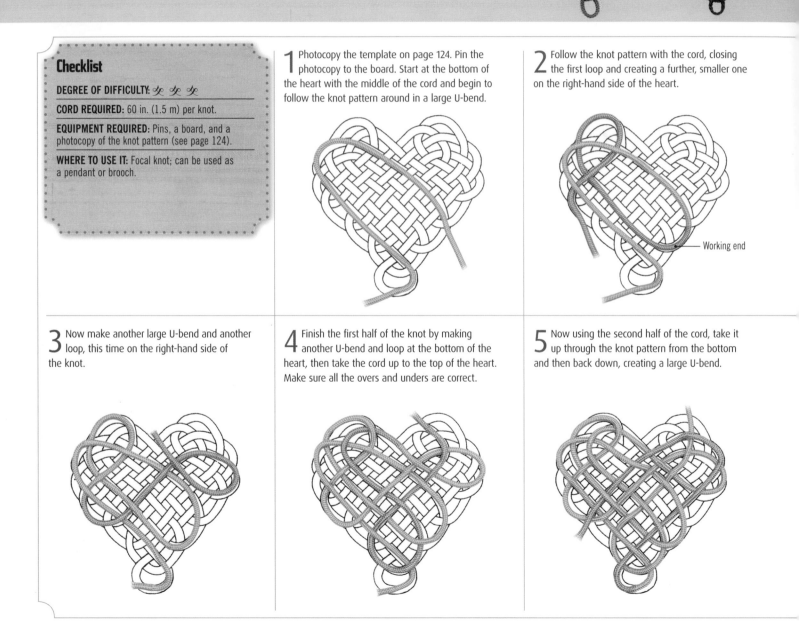

Checklist

DEGREE OF DIFFICULTY: ✄ ✄ ✄

CORD REQUIRED: 60 in. (1.5 m) per knot.

EQUIPMENT REQUIRED: Pins, a board, and a photocopy of the knot pattern (see page 124).

WHERE TO USE IT: Focal knot; can be used as a pendant or brooch.

1 Photocopy the template on page 124. Pin the photocopy to the board. Start at the bottom of the heart with the middle of the cord and begin to follow the knot pattern around in a large U-bend.

2 Follow the knot pattern with the cord, closing the first loop and creating a further, smaller one on the right-hand side of the heart.

Working end

3 Now make another large U-bend and another loop, this time on the right-hand side of the knot.

4 Finish the first half of the knot by making another U-bend and loop at the bottom of the heart, then take the cord up to the top of the heart. Make sure all the overs and unders are correct.

5 Now using the second half of the cord, take it up through the knot pattern from the bottom and then back down, creating a large U-bend.

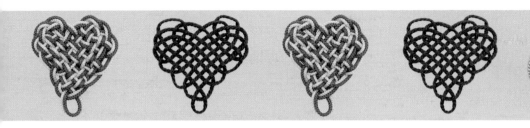

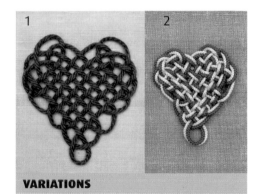

6 Pass the cord back through the knot, going up to the top, creating a loop at the top before going through the knot to the left-hand side. The cord follows a consistent repeating over, under pattern.

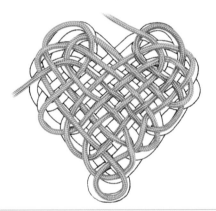

7 Create a final loop and then bring the cord through the knot to the top of the heart. Carefully check that all the overs and unders are correct.

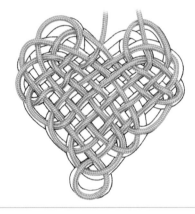

8 Double up the knot by passing a second cord around the knot, following the exact pattern of the first cord and ensuring the cords lie parallel.

9 Unpin the knot. It will be obvious if any of the over and unders are wrong as the cords will pop up. Tighten the knot by carefully pulling the cords through the knot to tighten any gaps.

VARIATIONS

1 Flat, stiff cord allows the knot to be left more open.

2 Two colors with a longer bottom loop.

Celtic square knot

Celtic square knots were traditionally used by early Christian monks to fill designs for embellishing manuscripts. This knot can be doubled, and like many flat knots, looks attractive when a second color is used.

Checklist

DEGREE OF DIFFICULTY: ✂ ✂

CORD REQUIRED: 20 in. (50 cm) per knot.

EQUIPMENT REQUIRED: Pins and a board.

WHERE TO USE IT: Focal knot; can be used with a pendant.

1 Create a large elongated loop, as shown, taking the cord over itself.

2 Now make a loop at the top of the knot and then pass the cord down through the knot.

— Working end

3 Make a U-bend at the bottom of the knot and pass the cord back through the knot to the top, going under, over, under, and over the cord already pinned down.

4 Complete the square knot by passing the cord back down to the bottom of the knot.

5 Run a second cord alongside the first one, exactly following the pattern of the knot to double it. Tighten the knot by gently pulling the cords through it.

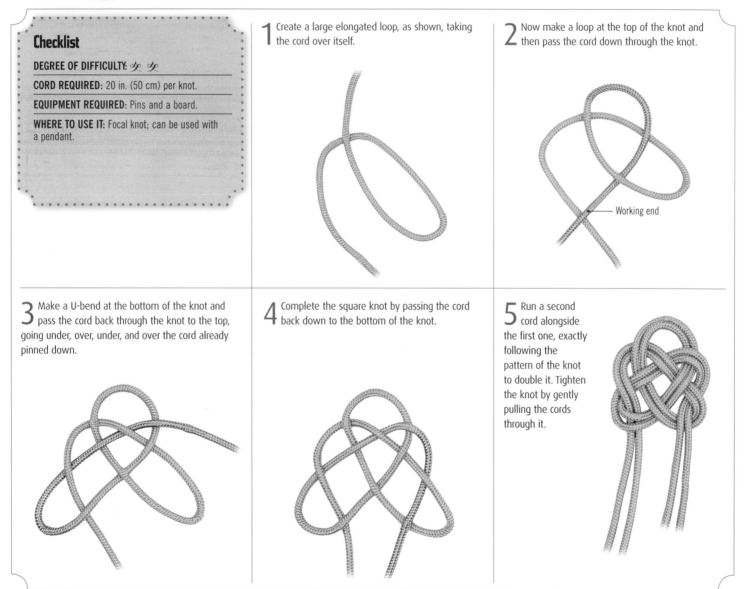

Plum blossom knot

This knot is named due to its similarity to a tree blossom. It is a pretty knot and looks attractive tied with both a single cord or doubled with a second cord, particularly if doubled with a complementary color.

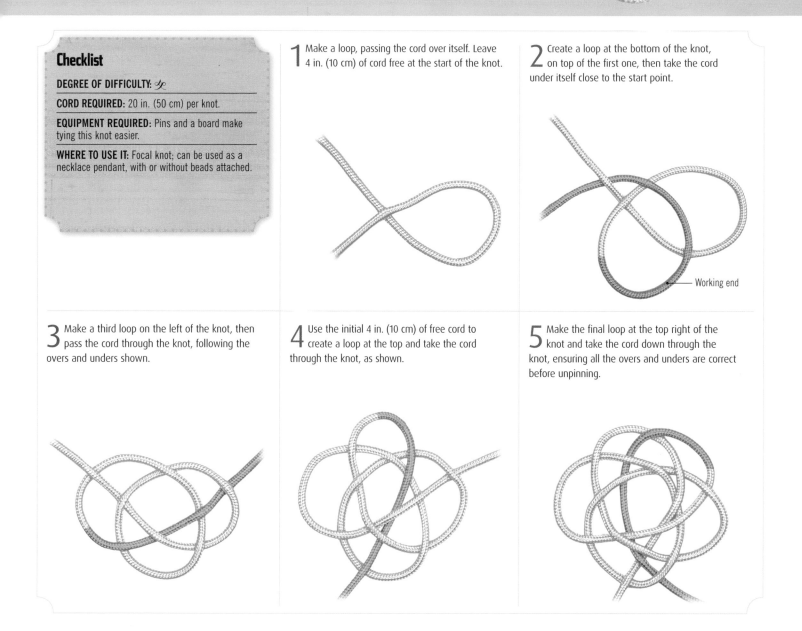

Checklist

DEGREE OF DIFFICULTY:

CORD REQUIRED: 20 in. (50 cm) per knot.

EQUIPMENT REQUIRED: Pins and a board make tying this knot easier.

WHERE TO USE IT: Focal knot; can be used as a necklace pendant, with or without beads attached.

1 Make a loop, passing the cord over itself. Leave 4 in. (10 cm) of cord free at the start of the knot.

2 Create a loop at the bottom of the knot, on top of the first one, then take the cord under itself close to the start point.

Working end

3 Make a third loop on the left of the knot, then pass the cord through the knot, following the overs and unders shown.

4 Use the initial 4 in. (10 cm) of free cord to create a loop at the top and take the cord through the knot, as shown.

5 Make the final loop at the top right of the knot and take the cord down through the knot, ensuring all the overs and unders are correct before unpinning.

Guinevere knot

Even though it is a large, impressive-looking knot, it isn't that hard to tie so long as the overs and unders are correct. Double this knot with a cord in a complementary color for a lovely subtle effect.

Checklist

DEGREE OF DIFFICULTY: ✺ ✺ ✺

CORD REQUIRED: 60 in. (1.5 m) per knot.

EQUIPMENT REQUIRED: Pins, a board, and a photocopy of the knot pattern (see page 124).

WHERE TO USE IT: Focal knot; can be used with a pendant.

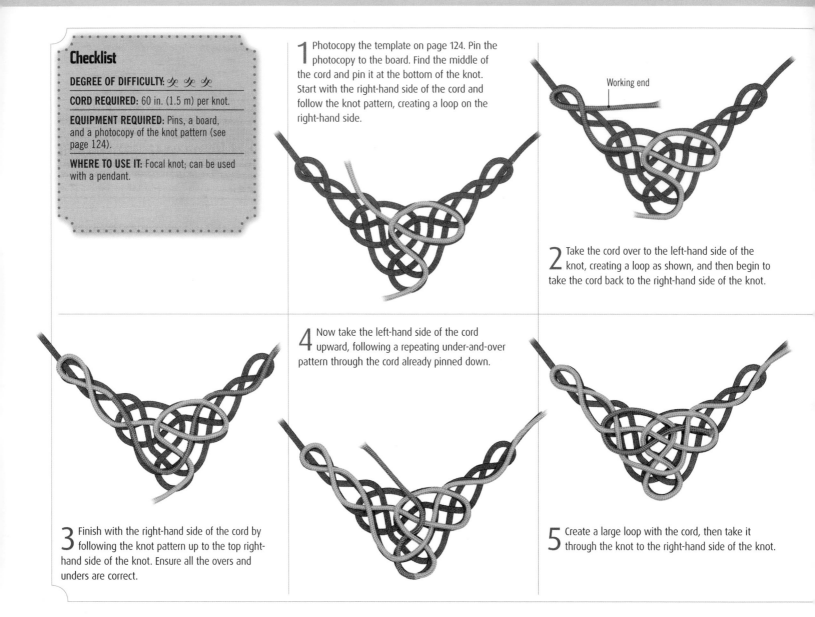

1 Photocopy the template on page 124. Pin the photocopy to the board. Find the middle of the cord and pin it at the bottom of the knot. Start with the right-hand side of the cord and follow the knot pattern, creating a loop on the right-hand side.

Working end

2 Take the cord over to the left-hand side of the knot, creating a loop as shown, and then begin to take the cord back to the right-hand side of the knot.

3 Finish with the right-hand side of the cord by following the knot pattern up to the top right-hand side of the knot. Ensure all the overs and unders are correct.

4 Now take the left-hand side of the cord upward, following a repeating under-and-over pattern through the cord already pinned down.

5 Create a large loop with the cord, then take it through the knot to the right-hand side of the knot.

6 Create a loop around the cord end on the right-hand side, then pass the cord through the knot, following the repeating over-and-under pattern to the bottom of the knot.

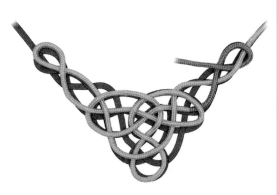

7 Complete the knot pattern by taking the cord up to the left-hand side of the knot, going through the loop created with the previous half of the cord. Ensure all the overs and unders are correct.

8 Double the knot with a second cord by passing it around the knot pattern, exactly following the path of the original cord, making sure the two cords don't twist around each other.

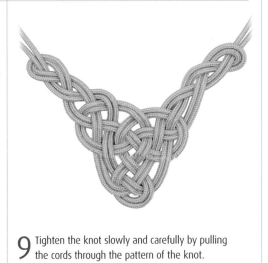

9 Tighten the knot slowly and carefully by pulling the cords through the pattern of the knot.

Jewelry projects

The projects in this section are intended to give
you some ideas for using and combining some
of the knots in the directory to make necklaces
and bracelets, incorporating different
materials and beads.

Donut necklace

The donut necklace is a macramé classic. The centerpiece is a donut-shaped focal bead and a simple sequence of knots follows. This version is a bit more complicated, including the Josephine knot, which is so pretty.

Materials

4 x 8-ft. (2.4-m) lengths of 7-ply black-waxed linen
1 donut centerpiece bead
Board
Pins
11 accent beads in varying sizes
Epoxy glue
Scissors

Choose fancy-edge flat beads to match your donut bead.

1 Take all four strands of waxed linen, fold them in half, and thread them through the hole of the donut bead to mount the start of your necklace using a lark's head knot (see page 56). Once completed, tie an overhand knot with all the strands. Secure the bead and material to the board with pins. You now have eight strands to work with. Separate them into two sets of four for each side of the necklace.

2 The first knot in the sequence is a Josephine knot (see page 59), tied about ½ – ¾ in. (1.3–2 cm) up from the overhand knot just tied. Tie one on either side of the necklace.

3 Leave another ½ in. (1.3 cm) of space before tying the next set of knots. The accent beads will be added at this time (reserve one of the smaller beads for the clasp). The sequence is as follows: tie an overhand knot, add two beads, tie a square knot (see page 55), add another bead, tie another square knot, add two more beads, tie another square knot. Repeat on the other side of the necklace.

4 Leave at least ½ in. (1.3 cm) of space before tying another overhand knot. Repeat on the other side.

5 Tie another Josephine knot 1 in. (2.5 cm) up from the overhand knot on either side of the necklace.

6 Tie another overhand knot about 1 in. (2.5 cm) from the last knot and then a length of repeating half knots (see page 54)—also known as twisting knots. Tie at least 12 to 14 knots to get a couple of twists. Finish with another overhand knot and repeat on the other side of the necklace.

7 Complete the necklace by making the clasp. Thread on the reserved bead and secure it tightly in place with an overhand knot on either side of the bead. On the other side of the necklace, tie another overhand knot a little bit up from the last one. There should be enough room between the knots for the bead to slip through but not so much that the bead slips out. Separate the strands between the knots to allow the bead to go through. Glue the knots and trim close once the glue has dried.

An accent bead and a cord loop form the clasp.

Half-hitch bracelet

This simple bracelet is made with a half hitch knot that is repeated, forming a natural twist. When choosing your beads, remember that the holes need to be able to fit however many strands of material you're threading through them. It's a good idea to bring the material with you when searching for the beads.

Materials

2 x 24-in. (60-cm) lengths of beige synthetic suede
2 copper split jump rings
Board
Pins
6 glass beads
Epoxy glue
Scissors
1 copper toggle clasp

1 Tie the two strands of synthetic suede to one of the jump rings. Secure the jump ring and materials to the board with a couple of pins. Thread on the first bead.

2 One strand is the holding thread and the other is the working thread, which is the one that knots around the other. Tie seven half hitch knots (see page 58). Note the twist that starts to form (you may need to adjust the strands to accommodate the twist). Thread another bead on both strands.

3 Take the shorter of the two strands and make this the holding cord, and use the longer piece to tie seven more half hitch knots. Thread on another bead and continue to repeat the process until the approximate length of 6 in. (15 cm) is reached, depending on your wrist size.

4 Finish the bracelet by tying the ends with an overhand knot to the other jump ring. Glue the end knots and allow to dry. Once dry, trim the ends and attach the toggle parts to each jump ring.

Natural color glass beads with large holes match the synthetic suede.

Synthetic suede or genuine suede or leather could be used.

A loop and toggle closure finish the bracelet.

Triple-strand twist-knot bracelet

The repeated half knot is a favorite among knot aficionados. This macramé knot creates a beautiful texture. One of the best parts of macramé is the fact that you can use different materials and a variety of colors. Here's a fine example of an indulgence in color and texture—triple strand, all twisted, and in great colors.

Materials

2 x 12-in. (30-cm) and 2 x 4-ft. (1.2-m) lengths each of turquoise, olive green, and dark blue 4-ply waxed linen

Board

Pins

Scissors

Epoxy glue

Sterling silver lobster claw clasp

Sterling silver jump ring

1 Each section of color is created separately and when they are completed they will be joined together with the dark blue waxed linen. Repeated half knots (see page 54) are used to build these sections, which create the twists, until the approximate length of 6 in. (15 cm) is achieved, depending on your wrist size.

2 When each section is done, lay them next to each other, secure to the board with pins, and prepare to wrap all the strands with dark blue half knots. Once the knots are started, trim the excess waxed linen of the other sections, glue them together lightly so they hold, and when the glue is dry continue tying the half knots. Tie about eight knots. Using an overhand knot, tie the ends to the lobster claw clasp, glue and trim when dry.

3 Repeat on the other side of the bracelet. Tie the ends onto the jump ring, and glue and trim when dry. The finished length for this bracelet is 7½–8 in. (19–20 cm).

Any three matching or chosen toning colors could use a gold-colored clasp if silver doesn't match.

The three sections are worked together at the ends.

Double-strand half-hitch necklace

Multiple strands of thin braided or knotted waxed linen with beads tied into them look great. Using 2-ply waxed linen gives this necklace a rather delicate feel, but because it's waxed linen it's strong. When repeated, the half hitch knot twists and gives this necklace lots of texture.

Materials

2 x 8-ft. (2.4-m) lengths of ivory 2-ply waxed linen

2 x 8-ft. (2.4-m) lengths of red 2-ply waxed linen

2 brass charms

2 boards

Pins

18–24 seed beads

18–24 small turquoise heishi beads

20 medium turquoise heishi beads

14 brass rings

22–24 brass tube beads

16 small bone beads

2 brass split jump rings

Epoxy glue

Scissors

1 brass hook clasp

Antique charms work well with turquoise.

1 It's easier to work on two separate boards for each of the two necklace parts, this way you can go back and forth and make sure everything is balanced. When the parts are finished they will be joined together off the boards. Let's start with the ivory necklace: Fold the strands in half and mount them onto one of the charms using a lark's head knot (see page 56). Secure the charm to the board with pins.

2 Tie half hitch knots (see page 58) using one of the strands (the working cord), which ties around the other strand (the holding cord). Tie about seven to eight knots and then thread a seed bead, small turquoise heishi bead, or brass ring onto the working cord. Continue tying seven to eight half hitches, adding one of the three types of beads, alternating as you go. The material will start twisting. Adjust the strands as necessary. Once four sections of half hitches have been knotted and three beads attached, thread a brass tube bead onto each strand.

3 Note that one of the strands is now shorter than the other. That was the working cord, which is now the holding cord. This allows the material to be used equally. Repeat step 2 and continue until you've reached the desired length, approximately 10–12 in. (25–30 cm).

4 Repeat steps 2 and 3 on the other side of the necklace.

5 Start the red necklace. As with the ivory necklace, fold the two lengths of waxed linen in half and mount to the other charm with a lark's head knot. Secure the charm to the board with pins. Tie an overhand knot about 1–1½ in. (2.5–4 cm) up from the charm. Thread a bone bead, a brass tube, and another bone bead. Tie at least 1 in. (2.5 cm) of half hitch knots—about 20 to 25 knots in total. Thread a medium turquoise heishi bead, a brass tube, and another medium turquoise bead. Tie an overhand knot 1 in. (2.5 cm) up from that section, then tie an overhand knot and thread a bone bead, a turquoise bead, a brass tube, a turquoise bead, and a bone bead. Tie another 1-in. (2.5-cm) section of half hitch knots and follow with beads in this sequence: turquoise, bone, brass tube, bone, and turquoise. Tie another overhand knot.

6 The balance of the necklace on both sides is as follows: overhand knot, bead, overhand knot, 1-in. (2.5-cm) space, overhand knot, bead, overhand knot. The sequence of beads is as follows: bone, brass ring, medium turquoise, bone, medium turquoise, brass tube.

7 Now both necklaces need to be connected. Take all four strands on one side and thread them through a brass tube and tie to a jump ring using an overhand knot. Repeat on the other side. Glue the knots and trim when dry. Attach the hook clasp on one side.

Prosperity necklace

This elegant necklace combines a centrally placed prosperity knot balanced by coin knots on either side, separated by antiqued gilt spacer beads.

Materials

3 ft. 2-in. (1-m) length of 1/16-in. (2-mm)Korean knotting cord

4 x 1/4-in. (6-mm) round antiqued gilt beads with 1/16-in. (2-mm) holes

1 x large glass flower pendant, 2 1/4-in. (6-cm) long

2 x gilt spiral cord ends

1 x gilt lobster-claw catch

Chain-nose pliers

Epoxy glue

1 Fold the cord in half and thread on the pendant. Tie a prosperity knot (see page 37) with the pendant at the top in the middle. Adjust the knot, keeping the pendant in the middle of the cord as much as possible and leaving it just loose enough to allow some light between the loops, as this shows off the pattern.

2 On one side, thread on a gilt bead, then make a double coin knot (see page 34). Adjust this knot to sit next to the bead, leaving it a little loose as before.

3 Repeat with a second bead and second coin knot.

4 Repeat the last two steps on the other side. Trim the loose ends at either side to match and to shorten the length if you prefer a shorter necklace. Glue the ends and slide the open side of the spiral cord ends over them. Squash the last loops of the spirals with pliers to secure these fittings (see page 21).

5 Twist the loop at the top of one end up, so that the catch will clip into it easily, and open the other end's loop. Place the catch on it and close it like a jump ring (see page 19).

Glass beads can be used instead of antique spacer beads.

Lobster-claw catch

Antiqued gilt beads

Spiral cord ends

In this variation, green cord is used instead of orange, and different beads are chosen to complement the new colorway.

Plafond earrings

This elegant Chinese knot (see page 39) was designed after the decorative centers of ceilings in Chinese palaces and temples. Here the knot forms the centerpiece of four very different earring styles.

Materials (red pair)

2 x 10-in. (25-cm) lengths of ¹⁄₁₆-in. (2-mm) Korean knotting cord

Pair of flat pad or cup-and-post ear studs

Epoxy glue

Tie a plafond knot (see page 39). Choose the neatest side of the knot and lie it face-down on your work surface. Repeat for the other earring. Cover the back of the knots with glue, enough to push the pad or cup of the ear fitting into it. Allow the glue to dry completely, then trim off the loop and loose ends from both knots so closely that the ends cannot be seen.

Materials (purple pair)

2 x 14-in. (35-cm) lengths of ¹⁄₁₆-in. (2-mm) Korean knotting cord

24 x ¼-in. (6-mm) cube silver beads with at least ¹⁄₁₆-in. (2-mm) holes

Pair of silver fish-hook ear wires

Epoxy glue

Thread four beads onto the cord and put them in the middle of the length. Tie a plafond knot (see page 39) with these beads in the loop, adjusting the length of the loop so that two beads sit on either side of it with as little cord as possible showing between them. Thread four beads onto each loose end and tie an overhand knot to hold them in place. Trim the ends to around ½ in. (1 cm) and fray the outer layer of the cord by running the end of an ear wire or similar through it. Push up the frayed part so you can trim away the white middle so that it cannot be seen.

Materials (blue pair)

2 x 16-in. (40-cm) lengths of ¹⁄₁₆-in. (2-mm) Korean knotting cord

Pair of silver ball ear studs with loops and butterfly backs

4 x ¾-in. (2-cm) long silver cones with ½-in. (1-cm) openings and at least ¹⁄₁₆-in. (2-mm) top holes

Epoxy glue

Tie a plafond knot (see page 39) and adjust the loop to be about 1½ in. (4 cm). Trim the loose ends to about 2¼ in. (6 cm) each and thread on the cones, narrow end first. Tie an overhand knot as near as possible to the ends of these cords and add a spot of glue. Pull the cones down over the glued knot. Make the other earring, matching the lengths.

Materials (brown pair)

2 x 14-in. (35-cm) lengths of ¹⁄₁₆-in. (2-mm) cotton cord

12 x ¼-in. (6-mm) round gilt beads with at least ⅛-in. (3-mm) holes

2 x ⅝-in. (1.5-mm) roundel-shaped, metal-lined glass beads

Pair of gilt fish-hook ear wires

Epoxy glue

Tie a plafond knot (see page 39) and adjust the loop to be about ¾ in. (2 cm). Thread three gilt beads, one glass bead, and another three gilt beads onto one loose end, then thread the other end through in the opposite direction. Put glue on one of the ends from ¾ in. (2 cm) to 1 in. (2.5 cm) from the main knot, then pull the two ends up so that the beads make a loop. The glue will fix the two ends together in the middle of the knot when it is dry. Wipe off any excess before it sets. Make the other earring in the same way, and when both are dry trim off the ends as closely as possible to the beads.

Silver cones and cube beads offset the smooth, matt cord.

Square-knot bracelet

The square knot is used for the main body of this simple and very cute bracelet, which is versatile and easy to create and can be made using a multitude of materials. Waxed linen, silk rattail, suede, hemp, wool, cotton, and leather lace could have all been used here. A pretty handmade glass flower bead is the focal point.

Materials

1 x 18-in. (45-cm) length of turquoise leather lace

1 x 36-in. (90-cm) length of turquoise leather lace

1 x 24-in. (60-cm) length of turquoise leather lace

1 flower bead

3 small coordinating accent beads

Board

Pins

Sticky tape

Epoxy glue

Scissors

Choose accent beads that coordinate with the focal bead.

1 The flower bead and one of the coordinating accent beads make up the centerpiece of this bracelet. String them onto the holding cord, which is the 18-in. (45-cm) length of leather lace. Thread the flower bead onto the center of the lace, then thread one of the accent beads onto the lace, threading back through the center of the flower to secure in place. Make sure the beads are centered on the lace and pull the accent bead tight to secure the flower bead. Secure the lace to the board with pins through the flower bead and tape down the ends of the leather.

2 Tie the 36-in. (90-cm) length of leather lace onto the holding cord 12 in. (30 cm) above the flower bead. Tie about five to six square knots (see page 55), which should bring you right above the flower bead. The next knot should start on one side of the flower and finish on the other side. This will really secure the flower bead in place. Tie another five to six square knots on the other side of the flower.

3 Flip over the bracelet and tie a knot to finish off this section. Glue the knot and trim when dry.

4 Create the closure of the bracelet with the 24-in. (60-cm) length of leather lace. Remove the ends of the holding cords from the board, cross them over each other and then secure them to the board with tape. They will be behind the focal section of the bracelet. Tie the 24-in. (60-cm) length of leather lace at the point where the two holding cord ends cross together, tying to both of them. Do not tie too tightly since you'll want the holding cords to be able to slide through to adjust the bracelet when it is put on or removed. Tie four complete square knots.

5 Flip over and tie a knot on the inside of this section as you did with the focal section. Glue and trim when dry. It's very important that you don't accidentally cut the holding cords. Tie a small accent bead at the end of each of the holding cords. These will serve as decoration but also keep the cords from sliding out when adjusting the bracelet.

The third group of square knots creates the sliding closure of the bracelet.

Resources

On these pages you will find templates to photocopy for the Uranus knot (see page 74), heart knot (see pages 102–103), and Guinevere knot (see pages 106–107). Also featured are lists of suppliers and other useful references.

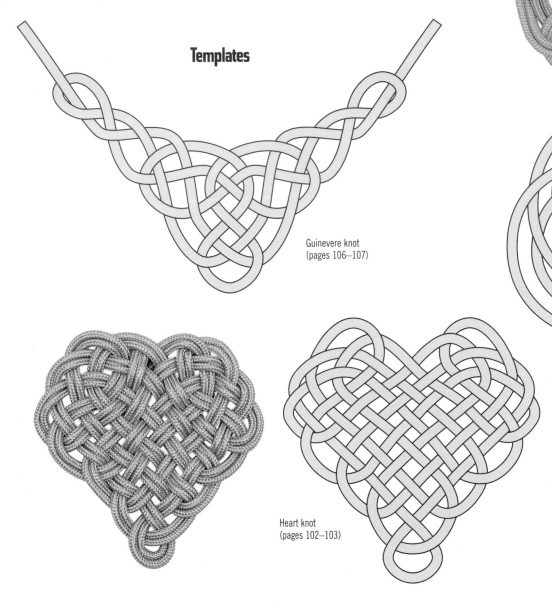

Templates

Guinevere knot
(pages 106–107)

Uranus knot
(page 74)

Heart knot
(pages 102–103)

Bead hole size

The most important factor when choosing beads is the hole size. Due to most cords being at least 1 mm thick you will need to ensure the cord fits through the beads. There is little point buying beautiful beads that you are unable to use because your cord is too thick to pass through the holes. Try a selection of beads with the cord to be used as not all beads have uniform-sized holes.

1 mm

1.5 mm

2 mm

2.5 mm

3 mm

3.5 mm

4 mm

Cord widths

Cords come in many different widths so you should bear this in mind before embarking on a project, especially if you are using beads, as you'll need to make sure the cord fits through the bead holes. Fine cords are well-suited for making knotted jewelry, while thicker cords are perfect for making larger ornamental knots.

1 mm
1.5 mm
2 mm
2.5 mm
3 mm
3.5 mm
4 mm

Suppliers

Knotting cord

www.satincord.com
(wide selection of knotting cords, findings, beads, and tools)

Beads

www.firemountaingems.com
(large selection of beads, including semiprecious beads and pearls)

www.beadcats.com
(large selection of beads and beading supplies)

www.beadinpath.com
(vintage and contemporary beads and crystals)

www.fusionbeads.com
(large selection of beads, findings, and stringing materials)

www.shipwreckbeads.com
(large selection of beads and beading supplies)

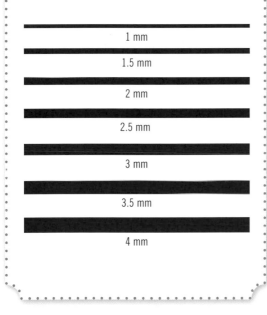

Index

Acknowledgments

Quarto would like to thank the following artists for kindly supplying projects for inclusion in this book:

Cathi Milligan: p.110, p.112, p114, p.116, p.122
Elise Mann: p118, p120

All step-by-step and other images are the copyright of Quarto Publishing plc. While every effort has been made to credit contributors, Quarto would like to apologize should there have been any omissions or errors—and would be pleased to make the appropriate correction for future editions of the book.

With special thanks to The Satin Cord Store for supplying knotting cords and Fire Mountain Gems and Beads for supplying beads for photography.